Conversations with James Joyce

CONVERSATIONS
WITH JAMES JOYCE

Arthur Power

Edited by Clive Hart

The University of Chicago Press

The University of Chicago Press, Chicago 60637

89 88 87 86 85 84 83 82   1 2 3 4 5

Library of Congress Cataloging in Publication Data
Power, Arthur.
   Conversations with James Joyce.

   Reprint. Originally published: London:
Millington, 1974.
   1. Joyce, James, 1882–1941—Interviews. 2. Joyce, James, 1882–1941—
Knowledge—Literature. I. Joyce, James, 1882–1941. II. Hart, Clive.
III. Title.
[PR6019.09Z7824 1982]   823′.912   82-6935
ISBN 0-226-67720-6 (pbk.)   AACR2

Foreword

While patient research has clarified many of the more recondite sources on which Joyce drew for the composition of his books, it has always been far from easy to determine how much of the main stream of European literature he had absorbed or what his literary tastes and opinions were. After his earliest adult years he wrote virtually no criticism, nor was he inclined to speak openly to the journalists and casual acquaintances who repeatedly sought to discover his views. Only a few friends were privileged to know anything of the real personality behind the courteous façade, friends who, with rare exceptions (like Hemingway), were not themselves literary men. Stuart Gilbert had been a judge; Frank Budgen was a painter; Arthur Power, a man of general culture and an art critic more or less by accident, was one of the even smaller number who succeeded in engaging Joyce in repeated and sustained conversation about literature and literary values.

Except for his sporadic and always highly specialized research into works of reference and comparatively rare books (much of it, in any case, carried out for him by willing amanuenses) Joyce was not often a great reader, and it is wise to be guarded in one's assumptions about the depth of his literary background. Arthur Power's conversations with Joyce reveal facets of that background which were previously either veiled or almost unknown. Joyce's interest in, and knowledge of, the great tradition of Russian prose writing can be seen to be more profound than one might have suspected, while his high opinion of Eliot (sometimes disputed) is now shown to be beyond question. Joyce's comments on literary theory are less than exciting, and as always he seems to have avoided prolonged discussion of his own books. Special interest is nevertheless to be found in one or two remarks about *Ulysses* and 'Work in Progress', such as his response to Power's question about what happened between Bloom and Gerty MacDowell: 'Nothing happened between them. . . . It all took place in Bloom's imagination', a remark which may help, by slightly altering the status of the first half of the 'Nausikaa' chapter, to explain the rather different roles played by the girls three hours later, in the nighttown scenes.

Joyce and Power had a number of things in common. Both had left the Church at an early age; both escaped from Ireland, in which they found much to dislike. In the first chapter of this book, Arthur Power presents a refreshingly honest portrait of himself as a young man of direct and open character, eager, like Joyce, to immerse himself in a culture more exciting than anything his native country seemed able to offer. Although less disturbed by his own developing personality than Joyce had been, Power was vividly aware of comparable tensions, and his account of the important moment of his First Communion, in which waning religious conviction confronted a growing sexual interest, presents some analogies with the adolescent experience of Stephen Dedalus. There were nevertheless strong temperamental differences which, as Power reports, occasionally led Joyce to mild displays of courteous exasperation at his young friend's insistence on the worth of the literature which he had undertaken to defend. After a slightly insecure start (an experience shared by many of Joyce's acquaintances) the friendship between Power and the Joyce family flourished in the twenties, for, apart from his personal attractiveness, Power had the important virtue, in Joyce's eyes, of being not only Irish but also loquacious. The days of the composition of *Ulysses* were over, and Joyce no longer needed Irish friends to confirm or modify his recollection of the topography of Dublin, but during the period of 'Work in Progress' he took every opportunity to listen to users of his native speech rhythms. In this Power served him well, and it seems that Joyce offered oblique thanks for his frequent friendly con-

6

versation by allowing him to double, in *Finnegans Wake*, with Frank le Poer ('Ghazi') Power, under the pseudonym 'gas-power'.

It is not only about literary topics that Power has something of value to say. He offers us many small insights into Joyce's daily habits and tastes in more mundane matters. Joyce's intense interest in the notorious Bywaters and Thompson case of 1922 provides hints for the possibility of further meanings in parts of *Finnegans Wake,* while the small vignettes which Power provides of Joyce and his family both at work and in more convivial circumstances are among the freshest to have been recorded. Very few of Joyce's Irish friends have been content to give us any extended account of the Joyce they knew; we are most fortunate that Arthur Power has now chosen to join their company.

CLIVE HART

Preface

In these conversations I have tried to reconstruct some of the talks I had with Joyce at different times from notes taken when I returned home after spending an evening with him.

I realize how inadequate much of it is, for much that was said has been forgotten or is inadequately expressed, while to give an impression of a man of such talent one would have to have talent equal to his own, as deep a consciousness of the social and psychological changes of his time as he had, and the same almost agonized gift for expressing it.

Also I see that being of a different temperament and opinion I have been too occupied with expressing my own point of view. All I can say is that that is how it was, since I was very talkative, while Joyce was naturally silent.

At the time these conversations took place I was a romantically inclined young man. My point of view has changed and coincides more with his, but such was it then, and such I have left it. In order to give the reader a clearer notion of my youthful personality and interests, I have prefaced the book with a brief account of my early life in Ireland, London and Paris.

A.P.

I

An early love of France must have been instinctive, for when
I was only fourteen I remember I persuaded my mother that
we should spend our Christmas holidays at Boulogne, arguing
that it would be a great opportunity to improve our French.
Crossing the Channel in a paddle steamer, we stayed at a
grumbling old hotel full of long passages, half-way up a wide
cobbled street on a steep hill. Opposite was the huge gothic
pile of the church where we went for Mass on Sundays, and
where I was immediately fascinated by the difference between
the ceremony I had known in England and Ireland, and that
in France. Inside the church a woman in a black knitted
shawl and a scarf on her head hired out wooden chairs to the
congregation, high backed, narrow and very uncomfortable,
which made kneeling a penance, and which scraped noisily
on the stone floor when turned around to be sat on for the
sermon. Then there were the small pieces of bread which were
handed around in a basket before the Communion; and that
round black silk bag on the end of the long stick, pushed
along in front of the worshippers to collect the sous; and
finally the magnificent beadle in his three-cornered hat and
gold-tipped staff, breeches and silk stockings, who strode
with such an authoritative air in contrast to the shuffling old
man in his ordinary black suit who used to function in the
church in Hampstead to which my school had been taken on
Sundays.

In my afternoons I used to wander about this foreign town

delighted to sit in the cafés listening to the babble of a foreign tongue of which I already understood something, and enjoying the different smells and tastes—much better smells and tastes than I had ever known before. I used to murmur to myself contentedly : ' This is what pleases me.' For I felt more at home here than I did in my own country, or in London.

At school in Hampstead I had only known the brutality of a horde of rough boys herded together, a violent and cruel world which I hated and in which I in turn was hated, so that my life was a wilderness from which there seemed to be no escape. I must have been unusually sensitive, which is a matter of regret since it gave others a great opportunity to prey on me, but some of my unhappiness was relieved one day when a young and attractive French mistress arrived. I immediately recognized her difference from the other prim-faced, raw-boned women who generally taught us. During the school walks I used to be allowed to walk beside her, while on her other side—and it seems to have been my fate all my life—was a tall blond boy called Rusborne who was the one she was really interested in, a silent and self-possessed youth who, in contrast to my ardent feelings, appeared to be quite indifferent to the affection she showed him.

Time has blurred my impressions, and now I only see my youth in a dim haze in which certain things stand out in cameo, while others have been lost. But my memory of Mademoiselle is one of the clearest, and she must have been attractive for I remember that young men, as we approached on our walks, used to lean against a brick wall as we passed, and say to her, ' Miss, can we join your school? '

On these walks she would talk about Paris, and I remember her descriptions of that gay and what seemed to me entrancing world. ' Ah, Paris ', she used to exclaim, ' that is something! Here it is nothing but fog and rain ', and she would go on to describe the Opéra where her father was a member of the orchestra—' une scène superbe—les loges . . .' filled with ' des gens chics ' for an opera by Verdi, or by Rossini. Then she would go on to describe the boulevards outside, a blaze of lights, the cafés crowded with people. She told me once, in a moment of bubbling youth and confidence, how when her young admirer came to the house she used to amuse herself curling his moustaches.

Her descriptions of Parisian life haunted my youthful imagination, stemming from a source I did not know, though it has since occurred to me that she must have stirred up some latent atavism since I am a Power, the Irish corruption of Poer—or Poher—the name of a family of Norman extraction who came over to Ireland centuries ago with Strongbow to settle around Waterford. Our family arms are of French origin—a stag bearing a cross between its antlers, taken from the legend of St Hubert, with the device underneath: *Per Crucem ad Coronam.*

Also the French origin of my family had been accentuated by my grandmother, a Miss Kane, who had been brought up in France and married my grandfather at the British Embassy in Paris. When she came to Waterford as a bride, the first thing she did was to break up the massive square Georgian front of the family mansion with a hexagonal two-tiered balcony of granite which jutted out in the semblance of a French château. She filled the hall and library with tapestries from Lyons and Courtray, ' The Descent of Persephone into Hades ' being one, ' The Meeting of King Solomon and the Queen of Sheba ' another. In the library she placed a very large tapestry of Neptune driving his sea-horses through a torrent of foam. The drawing-room she furnished with gilt-and-marble consul tables and a suite of Louis XVI chairs and settees upholstered with bergère prints of elegant shepherdesses in amorous conversation with equally amorous and well-dressed shepherds, all belonging to a world which is now much past, the aristocratic one.

My visit there when very young must have imprinted itself on my imagination in that period of life when all is surmise and dream: that old Georgian house with its tapestries, gilt furniture, mirrors, and the powder-blue bergère drawing-room suite, surrounded by lawns and shrubs, the river sparkling through the trees at the bottom of the field in front, trees which my grandmother had planted to hide the turbulent and ever-restless river Suir which, being tidal, was always in violent flood either up to Waterford city or racing down between its widely-spread mud banks as it foamed around the shipping buoys. I, who never knew her, was told that she had tried to shut it out.

It was to the French Mademoiselle that I gave my youthful and ardent affection. Twice in the week we used to be sent to the small Roman Catholic Church in Hampstead for instruction by an Irish priest, a handsome and saintly old man with a skin like parchment. We boys used to sit on a bench in the sacristy surrounded by the odour of incense, flowers and vestments. Even then I remember that I was not much impressed by his religious arguments, a fact which he noticed, sensing, as he must have done, a future rebel. I remember his stopping in the middle of his instruction, looking at me and saying, ' I know what is going to happen to you ', words which I still remember even though I did not then understand their meaning. I think he must have meant that I would not remain a believing member of the Roman Catholic community. I nevertheless looked forward to the great day with some excitement, hoping that, in the manner of a miracle, a sudden and mystical event would change my world, and bring me happiness.

At the ceremony Mademoiselle, the daughter of a musician, was to play the organ, and I remember my delight when she told me that she had chosen me to work the organ pump, offering the gallant excuse that I was a strong boy! My anticipated pleasure at being alone with her in the music loft before my First Communion was much reduced when I found I had to stand in a dark cobwebbed hole working an old-fashioned wooden handle up and down. Indeed, I was so bored and tired by it that I stopped several times so that the organ produced only a faint squeak, when she cried out, ' *Qu'est-ce qui se passe, alors?* ' More from love than from duty, I started to pump again, but this was certainly not my idea of preparation for the reception of the Holy Sacrament.

When the supreme moment arrived she called me out and we knelt together against the railing of the choir-loft looking down into the church, and then—a moment which I have remembered with great clarity over the years—as I rose to go down she kissed me on the mouth. I descended those narrow twisting stairs into the church to receive divine love with the imprint of human love on my lips—something which I have tried to repeat all my life.

I do not believe that any Englishwoman, or Irishwoman either (though that is more possible), would have acted as she did. But with the Latins, love is given a mystical quality. It is the outcome of generations of Roman Catholicism. When I was in Spain I used to be fascinated by the photographs of the young Spanish bridal couples I saw in the glass cases outside the photographers' shops: those dark-skinned, smooth-cheeked, serious-looking brides in their white lace mantillas surmounted with a tortoise-shell comb, and the bridegroom equally serious in his white shirt front and dress suit, so that one felt that there should be something sacramental in the consummation.

French marriages are more material, perhaps, but one feels nevertheless something of the same sanctity, and no doubt it was that which made Mademoiselle arrange for me to be with her in the music loft, and which led her to kiss me before I went down to communion—a finesse and intrigue which were particularly French.

Needless to say, I passed a day of supreme happiness for my hope that my world would be transformed had come true, although in a way which was more surprising than I had foreseen. I took care to remain alone as much as possible for the rest of that day in case some rough contact should disturb my feeling of sanctity. All this now seems a long way off, but these memories occur to me in retrospection to explain why I always had a vision of France, and above all of Paris, in the back of my mind.

It was not until the end of the First World War when, after innumerable medical boards, I was released from the Army, that I was able to realize my ambition. First I went to Italy, stopping in Florence, where I enjoyed the parties in the old palaces, the turbulent Arno flowing past their walls, and that famous house-bearing Jeweller's Bridge some hundred yards further down. The modern Florentines seemed as gay and amusing as their lively forebears.

Then I went on to Rome, where I visited museum after museum, but in the end these massive collections from the past depressed me, I, who wanted art to be a living thing, and to visit the studios where it was being created and meet the men who were creating it, with the paint still wet on their canvases, or in the case of a writer, to see his written corrections on the page. In other words, Paris was my objective.

So it was after this journey through Italy to Pisa, Florence and Rome, that at last I arrived in the French capital, worn out by the troublesome journey, for at that time everything in Italy was on strike. I had taken one of the rare overfilled trains in which officials spent their time going up and down the corridors abusing the passengers and kicking their luggage out of the way, piled as it was in the corridors. At last I tumbled out, thankful to have reached journey's end, and entered the Hôtel Terminus attached to the Gare St Lazare, a noisy bustling place rather like the station itself with its continual comings and goings, and the masses of luggage piled in the hall.

After exploring the city for a couple of days I decided to move out to the Latin Quarter where the students and, as I believed, the artists, lived. I was delighted to find an hotel in the Place de la Sorbonne facing the brilliantly lit Café d'Harcourt. The Hôtel Moderne, as it was called, was nothing much in itself except that in contrast to its name it was very old, with walls over a yard thick and small low-ceilinged rooms.

Not knowing a soul in the city, I used to wander about, walking everywhere, for Paris is too interesting to be hurried through in a bus or in the Métro. My evenings I spent on the Boulevard St Michel sauntering past the students' cafés. I looked around for artists, and though I saw an occasional black hat and flowing tie, they were few and scattered, and so eventually tiring of the brash energy of the students I would go for long walks up to the heights of Montmartre, where I knew that many great Impressionists had lived and had their studios. But the district of Montmartre had undergone great changes since their day, and the Boulevard Clichy was now full of sleazy joints, and expensive night clubs, where all America and Europe came to debauch themselves. It was only up on the heights around the Church of the Sacré Coeur that it was quieter, and from that height, leaning over a time-blackened wall, I could see all Paris lying below me bathed in light.

For some ill-defined reason I felt that the present-day artists had migrated elsewhere, for the people one saw sitting on the café terraces were obviously everyday folk or foreign and provincial pleasure seekers. I set off in search again, when one evening, travelling by chance past the tree-enclosed darkness at the top end of the Luxembourg Gardens, I entered a boulevard. Half-way along it I came on a café with lively-looking young men sitting on the terrace. As I sat down I overheard them, to my delight, discussing art, invoking the names of Degas, Renoir, and other artists. After a while I got into conversation with a lively and witty young man sitting at the next table who, as it turned out, was the sculptor Zadkine.

Perhaps because he had been brought up in England he was more sympathetic to the casual Englishman or Irishman than were the others, and one day he invited me around to his studio to see his work.

It was in an alley-way off the rue de Sèvres, and one entered through a wicket-gate across a vine-trellised courtyard. To the right was the entrance, and going up some steps one was enclosed for a moment in complete darkness before emerging on a landing to be faced with the door of his studio. A very large room, one corner of it was filled with a big window made up of innumerable panes, which always reminded me of the window in Rembrandt's picture of 'The Philosopher'. The wide floor was covered with Zadkine's sculptures. At the entrance stood a life-sized figure in wood, 'St John the Baptist'—hollow-cheeked and spare-ribbed, the man of locusts and honey; beside it was the figure of a nude girl in white marble enveloped in a shimmering wing—'Leda and the Swan'; in a corner against the right wall he showed me a

17

B

group of insect-like figures on a wood base bowed down in tribulation around a single recumbent figure—'Job and his Comforters'.

At the far end was a partition curtained off around a stove, its black pipe winding in snake-like contortions up the wall and finally disappearing out of the window. Set in this alcove were a table, some chairs, and a book-case filled with books.

Zadkine was an amusing and voluble conversationalist, who when he mentioned the word 'sculpture' gave it a peculiarly sensual inflection. Imprisoned in every piece of wood or stone, so he explained, he saw a recumbent form waiting to be released. In the neglected trunk of a tree he had seen this 'John the Baptist', and had released him; in that piece of white marble had been imprisoned his 'Leda and the Swan'. And, showing me the heavy chunk of wood he was then working on: 'In that', he declared, 'lives the most exciting deer you ever imagined, all the way from the Steppes of Russia, now to be released by me in my Paris studio.' Taking me to the window, he pointed into the courtyard where I could see two tall trunks of yellow wood carved into archaic figures, which had been stacked there because they were too large to fit into the studio. 'Gog and Magog', he declared, 'taken from the forest of Vincennes, and now enjoying the amenities of my beautiful courtyard. Sculpture should be a living thing. In the early morning it lies in sleep, then as the light strengthens it awakes, changing hour by hour until at mid-day it reaches its zenith like a rose, or like a woman in the moment of love. And then in the evening it closes up again like a flower, to be reborn in the first light.' While he talked he made me coffee in a Bedouin coffee-pot with a hammered brass base and a decorated spout.

I suppose that in spite of my desire to consort with artists and bohemians I had, perhaps owing to my army training, remained conventionally dressed, even carrying an umbrella at times.

'You are too heavily dressed', Zadkine told me with disapproval. 'Remember Nina', he continued, referring to a mutual friend of ours, an Englishwoman, 'every time I go out I see her wagging that nasty tail of hers up and down the boulevard. When we come to Paris we should lose our tails. They only get in the way.'

As I sat at the table beside the stove listening to him I noticed that he had a number of English books on his shelves: Swift's *Gulliver's Travels* and his brilliant, personal *Instructions to Servants*.

' I brought them from London ', he told me, ' for my books are my conscience; they must go where I go. It is all of my English life which is left for I am a Parisian now, or rather an international. We must lose our nationality, like our tails.'

Some days later, meeting me on the boulevard, he told me that he was going down to Savoy for a holiday where, he said, there were some old men ' who do marvellous things with snakes, and whom I wish to sculpt.' He asked me if I would like to rent his studio while he was away. Living as I was then in that hotel room in the Place de la Sorbonne I much preferred the attractions of his studio, one of the most bizarre and original in Paris. Shortly afterwards I moved in to take my place among that wooden population, a silent and fantastic company which in my imagination seemed always to be awaiting my return from the café at night. I used to spend my mornings in the curtained alcove reading Zadkine's books and experimenting with my own writing, while in the evening I used to frequent the Café Rotonde, and the Dôme, at the corner of the Boulevard Raspail and the Boulevard Montparnasse.

At that time there was a great stir in the artistic world, with the young men who had returned from the war showing their determination to create a new art to express modern life, for already Marinetti's famous Futuristic Manifesto was having considerable influence. He had declared that artists must create an art never conceived before, in which all truths learned in classes and studios must be abolished. ' The classical does not concern us. We are at the beginning of a new epoch '—a manifesto which in fact had a greater influence on the Left Bank intellectuals in Paris than it had in his own museum-cluttered Rome where it was first issued. There was considerable confusion, as at the beginning of all adventures, with innumerable false starts led by false leaders. Everybody was experimenting wildly, with novelty at a premium; every avenue and device was explored for ideas. One musician, a friend of Joyce's, composed a piece to be played by a hundred mechanical pianos as well as numerous other mechanical noise-making devices.

At that time the two chief artistic cafés were the Rotonde and the Dôme. The Rotonde was where the Latins and other Continentals used to congregate, Frenchmen, Spaniards, Russians and other Slavs. It consisted chiefly of a long, low-ceilinged room with the usual square marble-topped tables, and the walls hung with innumerable pictures. Through a passage was the traditional zinc-topped *comptoir* where one drank one's morning coffee and ate a *brioche* standing before the row of aluminium geysers in the din and clatter as the waiters called out their orders. Outside, the café terrace faced the Boulevard Montparnasse with the entrance to the Nord-Sud Underground station exactly opposite. The travellers who passed used to gaze curiously and cynically at the arguing intellectuals sitting on the terrace.

In winter the terrace was enclosed in a glass screen and charcoal stoves were placed at intervals, but in spite of this protection one was soon glad enough to go inside and sit in the main café. Here a continual stream of people entered and left: artists, models, viveurs and political revolutionaries. Trotsky frequented the districts before the 1914 war, and even at the time I speak of one would see groups of Spaniards huddled in a corner planning their future Civil War.

Immediately opposite, on the other side of the boulevard, was the Café du Dôme, the chief haunt of the English-speaking element: English, Irish, Americans, with a sprinkling of Danes, Swedes and Norwegians. Inside, the Dôme was more restricted than the Rotonde, for a large semi-circular *comptoir* took up most of its left side. The rooms at the back were dull and unimaginative, with high windows looking out on to the gloomy non-committal houses of the rue de Lambre, a street as depressing as the famous rue Morgue, consisting of a long line of dull houses which ended with the wall of the Montparnasse cemetery. The Dôme's wide and well-appointed terrace made up for its rather depressing interior, and here, as well as on the terrace of the Rotonde, the intellectuals used to collect in their crowds in the evening, so that as one approached this café from the distance at night, under the haze of lights, it looked as though it were a huge hive with innumerable swarming bees. Even in the afternoon there were always a number seated there, recognizable by their coloured shirts, sandals, and variegated head-gear when, apparently detached, they would remain for hours contemplating the busy boulevard before them. Indeed, in the hot and temperamental Paris afternoon their apparent indolence and detachment would sometimes so annoy passing van drivers and others, their nerves already frayed by the city traffic, that I have seen them pull up on the curb and pour abuse upon the half-conscious and immobile intellectuals. There was one man who used to drive up every evening and park his van with relish in front of the café terrace. On it was written, ' Extermination of Rats Undertaken '—that was evidently his business—for if the intellectual hates and despises the bourgeois, the latter in turn hates and despises the intellectual.

I cannot say that when I originally went to France I intended to get a job, in fact such an idea was repugnant to me. But although I preferred to frequent the cafés, *flâner* the boulevards, meet my friends and generally improve my mind, I suddenly found myself a sort of freelance art critic on the *New York Herald*.

In London, during the war, I had met the American sculptor, Jo Davidson. During the war, he and I used to frequent the Café Royal in Piccadilly which had a kind of fevered brilliance. Having lived my life with soldiers I knew nothing about artists, but now I decided that if I survived I would become one of them, for it was the only life, and they were the only people who interested me.

Jo Davidson was the first international artist I had met. I was fascinated by his wit, his vitality, and his freedom from all the shibboleths I had been brought up to revere but which in secret I used to make fun of, a thing which the conventionally minded sensed and made me pay for in their surreptitious way.

Calling for him in the evening at the book shop of Dan Rider, another jovial and pleasant person, I would walk with him to the Café Royal, and from there to some restaurant, often finishing up at a night club in the early hours of the morning, surrounded by a covey of belles attracted by Davidson's personality.

Now, the war over, he had established himself in Paris, where he was engaged in sculpting a huge 'Doughboy' to be erected in the American Cemetery. It was then that he suggested that he could get me a job on the *New York Herald*, for which I was to write a weekly article entitled, 'Around the Studios'. As he said, there was tremendous activity going on about which the public knew nothing.
—Exhibitions are all right, he pointed out, they are well advertised and people know about them, but there is no account of the daily work taking place in the numerous studios all around Paris.

So, undertaking this mission—for so I regarded it—I used to make visits to the different artists' studios, which in itself was an adventure, since they often lived in strange and inaccessible places, up crazy broken stairways and along perilous creaking balconies. If I thought a man had talent I would arrange to pay him a visit, and it was in this way that I first met Sola, the Spanish artist, who was later to be my friend, and it was from him I acquired my first Modigliani, a piece of sculpture.

One day, Davidson, who knew him, showed me some of Sola's drawings. Interested, I decided to make a call. He lived beside the Gare Montparnasse in a plain-faced red brick rambling building with a long, straight, narrow stair running like a ladder up to his studio, a big and bare high-walled room which was always plunged in obscurity. Indeed, with its stark walls and perpetual gloom, it reminded me of the cathedrals of Spain with their creeping lights, their stillness, and their detachment from the outside world.

Sola himself had that mixture of fire and melancholy which seems to be characteristic of his race. He was married to a French girl, a quiet and gentle creature who spent most of her day sitting by the iron stove knitting and taking an occasional drink of cabbage water to relieve her delicate digestion, the cure for all such ills according to her, and I still have a drawing of them sitting opposite one another portraying that grave and intimate austerity which seems to be an essential part of the Spanish character. The occasional exuberances of their famous fiestas and ferias have always seemed to me but temporary flashes of high tension bursting through their cast-iron conventionalism.

When I called on him it was already late in the evening, and as I sat talking to him my eye continually wandered to the far end of the studio where there was an old fashioned and massively built Breton cupboard, the kind that has been passed on through several generations of respectability. It had a lot of things piled in confusion on top of it, but what emerged from this penumbra of shadow and light, and constantly attracted my attention, was a stone head. Egyptian in style, the face was oval in shape and set on a long neck with a straight nose and a very small and full-lipped mouth. The eyes were elongated and smooth like pebbles, and full, soft cheeks had evidently been cut with a sequence of single hammer strokes which gave them a jewel-like quality. I asked Sola if he had done it.

—No, he said, that is by Modigliani. During the war I used to stand him meals. We were both hard up at the time but my parents used to send me money from Spain and so I had a little; enough, that is, for us both to eat, anyway. So one day he climbed up here carrying this head, and gave it to me as a present in return, I suppose.

For days afterwards that piece of sculpture haunted me, as the passion for a particular woman can haunt one, a constant obsession from which it is difficult to rid oneself. No doubt the casualness of its setting on top of the cupboard in the penumbra had originally stirred my imagination. Whatever the reason, I was determined to possess it.

At first Sola refused. It was a present from a friend and as such had sentimental associations. But as his financial circumstances were rather difficult he finally agreed, with reluctance, and after considerable bargaining the head was mine. When I came to carry it away I found it so heavy that I wondered how Modigliani had ever managed to carry it up those stairs by himself. Between us it took all our strength to carry it down and into a taxi, when I took it back to Zadkine's studio.

Some days later Sola called round to see me, and began to regret his sale, so that I had to soothe him as best I could. Forgetting his regrets, he walked around the studio looking at Zadkine's work and talking about Modigliani's theories on sculpture, telling me how Modigliani had hated Rodin's work —*un mouleur en plâtre* he had called him—for in Modigliani's opinion the essence of sculpture was that it should be hard, like a precious stone, ' emotion crystallized ', as he had said. —Was it not Brancusi who first persuaded him to take up sculpture? I asked him.

—That is so, he replied, though actually he did not care for Brancusi's own work. He thought that though he had a feeling for textures, for wood, stone and metal, he had no real creative power. Indeed, his abstractions, for which he was best known, often touched on the absurd, as for example his ' Torso ', which consisted of two short cylinders serving as two cut-off legs fitted into a larger cylinder. He also disliked the tombstone Brancusi carved in the Montparnasse cemetery, ' The Kiss ', those two seated figures with their arms wrapped around each other ' like ropes ', as Modigliani expressed it.

In Sola's opinion Brancusi's success was chiefly due to the fact that he was a good-looking man with an attractive personality which had helped him to become fashionable.

As he walked around the studio among Zadkine's forest-like figures, with that peculiar flat and square Spanish walk of his—a walk which was not unlike that of Picasso—he turned as if some sudden resentment had struck him, and said to me:

—You are a critic, aren't you? But, after all, a critic's point

of view is a personal one like anybody else's; the only difference is that you have the means of expressing it through the
press. But that does not make it more valid than anybody
else's opinion.

—It is a fate, I told him, like another fate. I have always been
very interested in art, but I did not particularly want to be a
critic. I have found out since that it is not satisfactory to
translate into words what is fundamentally an expression of
line, colour, and form.

Then, as we were talking, he stopped before some Goya
reproductions that I had pinned up on the wall by the door,
among which were the famous 'La Maja Vestida' and 'La
Maja Nuda'.

—I do not admire those as you do, he said. To me they
represent all that is most vile in man and woman. As we say
in Spain, 'all men are on the point of entering a bawdy
house', and I cannot look on them as works of art—that
woman lying on a couch with her arms behind her head the
better to show off her body.

—That she is sensual I admit, in the direct Spanish sense, I
said. She does not belong, as the French women do, to the
daughters of light; nor is she as the Italian women are, a
daughter of the moon. She is the daughter of darkness. But
as a nude you must admit that she is superb. Some nudes
have been painted too hard, and some again too fleshy, as
Rubens', but she is neither, for Goya laid stress on the texture
of her skin, which is fine, uniform, and delicate. Also on that
of her hair. The Egyptians believed that love lay in the hair,
and in the eyes. In 'La Maja Nuda' they are in both.

—It is her eyes I object to, said Sola. They are the eyes of a
houri.

Then, seeing that I was boring him,

—What do you think of Modigliani's nudes? I asked.

He shrugged his shoulders.

—They are very sensual. I came into his studio one evening
as he was finishing what is now known as 'The Great Nude',
and he asked me what I thought of it. 'It is a map of a naked
woman', I told him. 'That's what it is for', he replied

moodily, ' to enable me to find my way around ': and, disappointed at my criticism, he picked it up and turned it to
the wall. But really, that model stretched out for love, or
copulation rather, did not seem to me a work of art.

—I think you were wrong, I said, for she is very beautiful,
and that is all that matters. Only if she were ugly, in my
opinion, would it have been wrong to paint her like that.

II

The first time I met James Joyce was at the Bal Bullier. I had gone there one Saturday evening to meet Annette, the young blanchisseuse who used to call for my washing every week, a handsome self-willed girl who later became a model, and whose life ended in tragedy.

It was the fact, I think, that I lived in a studio that interested her in my lonely bachelordom, for while I talked with her she used to amuse herself by kicking the odd pieces of coal which lay in front of the stove across the floor, a subtle intimation that she did not think much of my domestic arrangements. She told me she used to go dancing every Saturday so I asked her to meet me at the Bal Bullier, a popular dancehall of the Montparnasse district which, like much of old Paris, has since disappeared, but then it stood at the top of the Boulevard St Michel in the Avenue de L'Observatoire opposite the Luxembourg Gardens.

The Bal itself was a large building and one entered down a flight of stairs, for the foundations were below street level. Inside it consisted of a wide dance-floor surrounded by a balcony supported on iron pillars, and underneath this balcony were placed rows of marble-topped tables and iron chairs. It had two orchestras, a brass one and a string one which played alternately at opposite ends of the floor, neither, as can be imagined, of a very high order, for it was chiefly frequented by the local shop-boys and girls, with a sprinkling of intellectuals who, tiring of the cafés, entered to find distraction and were pleased by its old-fashioned atmosphere and low prices. In its day it had been a fashionable resort, but being outmoded it had gradually declined except for one or two occasions during the winter when the big artistic balls organized by the different studios were held there. On these occasions it used to be completely transformed when the students from the studios erected small stages on the floor and gave burlesque performances during the intervals of the dance. The now deserted balcony was then crowded with supper tables, with all bohemian Paris packed on to its floor. But this night was one of its ordinary nights with only about thirty couples dancing.

As I entered I saw a party seated at one of the tables, one of whom I knew, a lady who was a friend of Jo Davidson. I took care to avoid them, for I had come there to meet Annette and not to pass my evening with intellectuals (my constant and recurring fate). I was excited at the idea of an evening with this handsome girl with whom, as a lonely man, I was already half in love, and would, if fates were kind, be fully in love with before the night was out. As time went on Annette did not appear, though I searched and re-searched that vast hall for her, so that in the end I despaired that she would keep her rendezvous. Anxious for some company to help me forget my disappointment, towards the end of the evening I passed by the table where the party was seated. A lady called me over and introduced me to a slightly built, finely featured man with a small pointed beard who wore thick lensed glasses—' Mr James Joyce ', she said. The introduction came as a surprise for I did not know that he was in Paris. The last time I had heard about him he was living in Switzerland.

While living in Dublin I had read *Dubliners*, and later I had read *A Portrait of the Artist as a Young Man*, but being at that time chiefly interested in romantic literature I had not been greatly impressed by his books. I was nevertheless intrigued to meet one of our most important authors, and I liked the man himself, his quiet sensitive manner and his old-fashioned courtliness, and I soon found myself sitting next to him. He asked if I came from Dublin, seemed pleased when I told him that I did, and asked how long had I left it and whom I had known there. These questions did not altogether please me, for I had gone to Paris to forget Ireland as a whole, and my native Dublin in particular.

Our conversation was interrupted by a young American woman at the table, Miss Sylvia Beach, who proposed that we should all fill our glasses and drink a toast to the success of James Joyce's new book, *Ulysses*. Towards midnight the party broke up, but as we stood on the boulevard outside, Joyce suggested that I should cross over with him to the Closerie des Lilas opposite for a final drink before we parted, when he told me of the difficulty he had had in finding a publisher for this new book, which had taken him eight years to write.

After that night I did not see him again for some time until I received a message through a mutual friend suggesting that I should call on him at an address in the rue de Rennes. So a couple of evenings later as I happened to be passing his flat on my way to a studio party in the Montrouge district I called in to see if he would accompany me. I believed then that an artist should be something of a bohemian, especially in the exciting circumstances which a city like Paris offered, and it had seemed to me, in the short time that I had met Joyce, that he led a very restricted and bourgeois life. I wanted to persuade him to come to this party, which was to be held in the studio of a Russian painter called Feder, whose place was out in the Montrouge district in a garden behind a block of flats. It looked more like a booth in a fair than an artist's studio, and had about five different entrances which in turn had been blocked up by each new tenant in an effort to keep out the draughts. One side of it had been torn badly, and the story was that a painter of animal subjects who had lived in it had had a lioness brought in. She had torn it down, it was said, in protest against ' having to pose in her skin '. In this studio Feder had a magnificent assembly of negro sculpture, one piece of which, a representation of the sun in yellow wood, displayed its pointed rays running down the whole length of the wall. He had also collected numerous dance-masks, exotic and macabre, and some musical instruments. A Russian Jew, he had escaped from the pogroms in Odessa to become a painter in Paris. A kindly and urbane soul with a gentle, cynical wit, he was an excellent host.

I thought that in such an atmosphere Joyce would relax,

have a drink, and talk with the girls, but I was badly received by the family, as I had arrived at his flat with my pockets full of bottles. Since Joyce's eyes were very weak at that time, he had been forbidden to drink, and they looked on me as the proverbial drunken Irishman inviting him out on a Celtic bash. Georgio, his son, stood over my chair with his legs apart as much as to say, ' When are you going to leave?' It was an awkward situation, and I decided to make out as best I could. Joyce, bending to the storm with a rueful smile, refused my invitation, while I, feeling the atmosphere so charged, was glad to make my escape. As I went down the passage Joyce accompanied me to the door and, as I passed out, standing with his back against the wall he said to me in a plaintive, but amused voice :

—You know I am an intelligent man, but I have to put up with this sort of thing—however, he commented with a smile, we will meet again soon.

At the time I thought he was a much bullied man, but when I got to know him and the family better, and to understand the serious threat to his sight, I changed my point of view. Shortly afterwards I met him again in the rue du Bac when he invited me back to his gloomy, iron-shuttered flat. I immediately became great friends with his family, and particularly with Nora, who realized that I had no wish to lead her husband into drinking bouts, that in fact I disliked drinking to excess.

Joyce, a restless man, was continually changing his abode, partly through circumstances no doubt, but also on account of his nature, and shortly afterwards he moved to a pleasant, airy apartment opposite the Eiffel Tower, where I used to visit him frequently.

I always took care not to call at his flat until the late afternoon, when he used to come into the room from his study wearing that short white working-coat of his, not unlike a dentist's, and collapse into the armchair with his usual long, heart-felt sigh. As often as not Mrs Joyce would say to him, —For God's sake, Jim, take that coat off you!

But the only answer she got was his Gioconda smile, and he

would gaze back humorously at me through his thick glasses. Later in the evening it was his normal habit to dine at ' Les Trianons ', a smart restaurant opposite the Gare Montparnasse. Once I met Marie Laurencin there when she stopped on her way out to speak to Joyce. A great admirer of her work, I was fascinated by those delicate and supersensitive young girls of hers. But to my surprise, I, who had imagined her to be like them, found her heavily built and rather masculine-looking— a woman who, according to gossip, preferred *hommes de sport* for her companions, footballers and racing cyclists.

—Monsieur Joyce, she told him, I want to do a portrait of your daughter. Tell her to come on Thursday next, at eleven o'clock.

I believe that when Lucia did turn up, Marie Laurencin was lying in a darkened room complaining of a headache from the previous night's *bombe*. She put off the meeting to a later date, and so I never saw the portrait, which is a pity, since Lucia, with her sensitive bearing and that squint of hers, would have been Marie Laurencin's typical subject.

After returning to his flat in the Square Robiac, Joyce would settle down in a sympathetic and social mood. Here in the evening, with his favourite bottle of white wine, ' St Patrice ', at his elbow, a wine he discovered while on holiday in the south of France, we used to discuss many things, but the main subject of our conversation was naturally our common interest in literature. In the ordinary sense Joyce was not a conversationalist. In fact he was remarkably taciturn, ' silence, exile and cunning ' being his three vaunted weapons, though I must say I never saw any evidence of the third quality, for he was singularly open-hearted and devoid of guile, except perhaps that all silent men seem more cunning than do talkative ones. In our discussions I spoke much more than he, and I think it was my argumentativeness which strangely enough cemented the friendship between us.

Joyce had lent me the manuscript of *Ulysses,* which I carried in a bulky parcel tied up in brown paper, across the taxi-ridden streets back to my studio in constant fear that I should be run over and the manuscript lost. But when I sat down to read it I found myself confused by its novelty and lost in the fantasia of its complicated prose, not knowing if a thing had really happened or was just a Celtic whorl. In fact I later irritated Joyce by enquiring into the details of what actually occurred during Bloom's encounter with Gerty MacDowell on the beach.

—Nothing happened between them, he replied. It all took place in Bloom's imagination.

It is said that when H. G. Wells put down the loosely bound first edition, with pages falling all over the place, he felt that he had suppressed a revolution; but I knew that one had been launched. Taking for his subject his native city, which once he had evidently hated, but which now he had re-found to cherish, Joyce had created a new realism, in an atmosphere that was at the same time half factual and half dream.

In regard to its well-known analogy with Homer's *Odyssey,* an analogy which at the time I questioned, I remember Joyce choosing as an example the 'Sirens' episode which takes place in the Ormond Bar on the quays. He compared the barmaids with Homer's Sirens, pointing out that the barmaids, with careful hair-do, make-up, and smart blouses, looked well only to the waist, and that below the waist they wore old stained skirts, broken and comfortable shoes, and mended stockings. Again, when I once admired the phrase ' *Thalatta! Thalatta!* She is our great sweet mother ', he looked across at me and said ' Read what I have written above : " The snotgreen sea. The scrotumtightening sea. " '

Whereas Homer's *Odyssey* describes prancing horses, handsome men and fair women, gods and goddesses, Joyce's *Ulysses,* as we know, is laid in tattered streets among blowsy women and in jostling bars, culminating in the episode of ' Nighttown '. I remember the brothel area faintly from my youth, a very fly-blown district including a number of thatched cottages in which every trick was practised, with a number of oldish women in black shifts running about. If you got up to talk to somebody, by means of some miracle only known to them you found, when you returned to your seat, that your whiskey had been changed back to water—

while in a back room there lay a peasant Venus with a religious lamp burning over the nuptial bed. Despite these sordid memories, it meant something to me that an Irishman from Zürich had arrived in Paris with a huge masterpiece, in the modern idiom, based on my native city. Indeed, it was perhaps pride in this achievement, rather than a reaction against Joyce's bourgeois life, that had really prompted me to try and bring him to studio parties, in order to show him off to my friends.

One evening we had an argument about the merits of Synge. Joyce knew him when he was living in the rue d'Assas but found him very difficult to get on with.
—He was so excitable, Joyce told me. I remember once going around to him and suggesting that we should spend the 14th July in the Parc de St Cloud. But Synge objected violently to the idea of spending the holiday, as he expressed it, 'like any bourgeois picnicking on the grass', and he refused to go. In fact there were such heated arguments between us that in the end I had to give up seeing him.
—And what do you think of his work? I asked.
—I do not care for it, he told me, for I think that he wrote a kind of fabricated language as unreal as his characters were unreal. Also in my experience the peasants in Ireland are a very different people from what he made them to be, a hard, crafty and matter-of-fact lot, and I never heard any of them using the language which Synge puts into their mouths.
—But he must have got it from somewhere, I said. I know that in the west of Ireland I used to hear marvellous phrases. I remember once asking a peasant on Costelloe Bay if there were many seals in it. 'Seals', he exclaimed, 'sure they do be lying out there as thick as the fingers of my hand, and they sunning themselves on the rocks'—a phrase which seemed to me to be pure Synge. And do you remember the speeches of Mary Byrne in *The Tinker's Wedding* when she talks about the great queens and they making matches from the start to the end, 'and they with shiny silks on them the length of the day, and white shifts for the night'?

C

—Now who ever heard talk like that? protested Joyce.

—The question is, I said, is literature to be fact or is it to be an art?

—It should be life, Joyce replied, and one of the things I could never get accustomed to in my youth was the difference I found between life and literature. I remember a friend of mine going down to stay in the west, who, when he came back, was bitterly disappointed—' I did not hear one phrase of Synge all the time I was down there ', he told me. Those characters only exist on the Abbey stage. But take a man like Ibsen—there is a fine playwright for you. He wrote serious plays about the problems which concern our generation.

—Ibsen, I exclaimed in surprise. I would not compare Ibsen with Synge, for to me there is something essentially ugly about those suburban dramas of his, about those boring people who live in mean surroundings, while Synge's are magnificent creatures in my opinion, living in communion with Nature, ' with the Spring coming up into the trees '; and ' a dry moon in the sky '; and ' a drink-house on the way to the fair ', grand and devil-may-care bodies in contrast to Ibsen's who pass their lives in consulting rooms, or attending board meetings; those frustrated bores who are the official and professional strata in any town.

—What about Dr Stockman in *An Enemy of Society*? Surely you admit that he was a fine character, remarked Joyce.

—He was brave, I suppose, in his own fashion, I admitted, a fine man even, but what a lamentable lack of poetry in the whole play; all that business about infected drains, leaking water-pipes, and the ' Hygienic Baths ' and ' lots of invalids '.

—You have not understood the play, Joyce objected, for the infected water supply and the leaking pipes you mention are all symbolical of what Dr Stockman was protesting against, ' that all our spiritual sources are poisoned '. Surely you must agree that Dr Stockman is a far finer character than any of Synge's and that a man fighting against the corrupt politics of his town is a finer theme than brawling tinkers, and half crazy ' play-boys '.

—I wonder, and wonder very much, I replied. Indeed if I

remember rightly Synge disliked the plays of Ibsen. He dealt with what Synge calls 'seedy problems' in joyless and pallid words but, as Synge says: 'in a good play every speech tastes of nuts or apples'.

Joyce shook his head.

—You have not understood him, he said, neither his purpose nor his psychological depth, as opposed to Synge's romantic fantasy; his brilliant research into modern life when he plumbed new psychological depths which have influenced a whole generation of writers. But whom has Synge influenced? Nobody but a few playwrights also trying to work for the Abbey, writing about provincial comics, characters from whom they hope to raise a laugh.

—Is it so wrong to be humorous? I said. In fact it is Ibsen's deadly seriousness which repels me and the fact that he saw life only as a battlefield for those dreary ideas of his.

—As I say, repeated Joyce, you do not understand him. You ignore the spirit which animated him. The purpose of *The Doll's House*, for instance, was the emancipation of women, which has caused the greatest revolution in our time in the most important relationship there is—that between men and women; the revolt of women against the idea that they are the mere instruments of men.

—And the more the pity, I replied, for the relationship between the sexes has now been ruined; an intellectualism has been allowed to supersede a biological fact, and the result is that neither is happy.

—The relationship between the two sexes is now on a different basis, but I do not know whether they are happier or unhappier than they were before; I suppose it depends on the individuals. But I do know that Ibsen has been the greatest influence on the present generation; in fact you can say that he formed it to a great extent. His ideas have become part of our lives even though we may not be aware of it.

—You are probably right, I said, in fact you are right. But I still dislike his dried up personality so much and the plays he wrote, that I cannot agree with you about him. For me language is all important, and that is why I admire Synge: for his splendid language.

—It is his language that I object to, replied Joyce, those long overweighted sentences, through which the actors have to stumble painfully, wondering, as they seem to do, if they will ever get to the end of them—long flowery speeches which hold up the action. It is a misuse of the stage. Take a dramatist like Sheridan. Look at his quick short sentences, primed and witty. There is no drooling about him.

—That is the actors' fault, I said, if they cannot manage them. In the case of Synge, they seem to me to run naturally if they are taken in the accent and mood of the people they are supposed to represent. They have dignity, passion, colour and personality. I hate the back-chat type of play. It can be very wearisome indeed.

—Drama is the art of significant action and except you are a Shakespeare you should not attempt to smother it in language as Synge does. In contrast, Ibsen's dialogue is always slim and purposeful. It must be Synge's romanticism which appeals to you.

—Maybe you are right, I replied, for the question is, has there ever been any worthwhile art produced which is not romantic?

—It depends what you call art, doesn't it? For in my opinion there are as many forms of art as there are forms of life.

—It is intoxication in one form or another, I said, to be always drunk, as Rimbaud puts it, drunk with life—is not that what an artist should be?

—That is the emotional aspect, said Joyce, but there is also the intellectual outlook which dissects life, and that is now what interests me most, to get down to the residuum of truth about life, instead of puffing it up with romanticism, which is a fundamentally false attitude. In *Ulysses* I have tried to forge literature out of my own experience, and not out of a conceived idea, or a temporary emotion.

—I think you wrote better when you were romantic, I said, as for example in *A Portrait of the Artist*.

—It was the book of my youth, said Joyce, but *Ulysses* is the book of my maturity, and I prefer my maturity to my youth.

Ulysses is more satisfying and better resolved; for youth is a time of torment in which you can see nothing clearly. But in *Ulysses* I have tried to see life clearly, I think, and as a whole; for Ulysses was always my hero. Yes, even in my tormented youth, but it has taken me half a lifetime to reach the necessary equilibrium to express it, for my youth was exceptionally violent; painful and violent.

—All one's life is painful and violent as far as I can see, I said. I was looking at an Italian clock in the window of an antique shop the other day, and written across the dial were the words *Every one hurts and the last one kills*.

—Every one hurts and the last one kills. That is good, Joyce remarked, I must remember that.

III

Joyce hated to go to any restaurant other than those few which he habitually frequented, and nothing would induce him to enter the well-known bohemian cafés of Montparnasse. When he did not go to the 'Trianons', he sometimes dined *en famille* at the Café Francis in the Place Francis which faces the Seine and the Eiffel Tower, and after a visit to the theatre he would call in there before returning home. Once I tried to break his normal habits by taking him to a restaurant near the Madeleine which specialized in Alsatian food and wine. Although it was exceptional, it put him into a difficult mood. On another occasion we went to a famous restaurant in Montmartre where as we waited for a table some Frenchman recognized Joyce and exclaimed in a loud voice that here was a genius. But since it was not his favourite 'Trianons' he was ill-at-ease. By the door I noticed a woman before whom all the men stopped and spoke in a particularly friendly manner, so that one wondered who she was, perhaps a famous actress or a singer. In the end we found that she was the manageress of a well-known *maison close* around the corner, and was thus a person of considerable importance in the neighbourhood, with information about the capabilities of the latest beauty on the market. As Joyce remarked, ' a reigning duchess would not have received more deference and attention.'

He hated anything to do with bohemians, and always showed contempt for their way of life. Once, when I asked where he liked to go for his holidays, he answered abruptly : ' To some place where honest people earn an honest living.'

He seemed to have a passion for an ordered life, and I thought it a reaction from his former life in Dublin, from the poverty and bohemianism of his youth, of which one heard various accounts from people who had known him at that time. One day, meeting his friends in the street, he told each of them that they must meet him again on the following Saturday at midday at the bottom of Grafton Street with a pound note in their pockets—a matter, he intimated to them, of the utmost urgency. On the following Saturday a number of them turned up.

—Have you all got your pound notes? he asked, and when they produced the promised money he said, now let us all go and dine at Jammet's.

(Jammet's being at that time Dublin's best known and most expensive restaurant, a few yards from their meeting place.) Such and other stories are told of Joyce's bohemian youth, but in Paris he lived the most ordinary life imaginable, remaining shut up in his flat during most of the day.

Once I wanted him to meet Jo Davidson, but the meeting was not easy to arrange for Joyce first made innumerable enquiries about him before he would agree to the meeting. I wanted to fix the Deux Magots on the corner of Boulevard St Germain as the meeting place, a café frequented by a few American writers such as Hemingway and some others, and by some of the local French bourgeoisie. But Joyce refused to go there, and made the appointment at a small café or bistro at the juncture of the rue du Bac and the Boulevard St Germain. There he sat waiting for us, a solitary and lonely figure on its deserted terrace, about three minutes' walk from the popular cafés where all his friends met.

Indeed, famous man though he was, the life he lived was, socially speaking, hermetically sealed. On one of those rare occasions when we were sitting in a wellknown café on the Left Bank, some American writers sitting at another table, one of whom I think he knew, sent over a message asking him to join them. He sent back a reply saying that he was with his wife and friends and regretfully refused. Everywhere he went he acted in the same detached manner. If, for instance, anyone he

came up to greet him in a restaurant, or at a theatre, or
 public place, he would quickly disengage himself and
 his isolation.

 hile one talked to him one could not but feel, at times,
that he was using the conversation as a sort of counterpoint to
his own thoughts, which ran in an altogether different vein
as he mentally composed ' Work in Progress '. One evening,
in a temporary moment of exasperation, I exclaimed as he
was serving me a drink at one of his parties :
—You are a cold man!
I will never forget his astonishment.
—I, a cold man? he repeated.
At the constant parties in his flat I admit that to some
extent a different man showed himself when, with his open-
handed Irish hospitality, friendly and relaxed, he moved
among his guests. These, incidentally, were at that time nearly
always the same people. They included Miss Beach, the
vivacious New Englander whose one absorbing interest was
Joyce and his works, and who gave the impression that she
was willing to be crucified for him on the sole condition that
it was done in a public place; Mlle Monnier, her friend; and
an American pair, the Nuttings. The first time I had met Mlle
Monnier was in one of those smart restaurants on the Champs
Elysées which stand among the trees near the Boissy d'Anglas.
A large, impressive woman, she was dressed that evening in a
black nun-like garment which completely mystified me until
I was told it was the official Communist attire. I must say that
it seemed to me strangely out of place in those surroundings.
But when she came to Joyce's parties she wore an ordinary
black dress, and always appeared to be one of those impassive
French who are frequent enough but who always seem out of
character. She had her wellknown book shop, ' Le Navire
d'argent ', in the rue de l'Odéon opposite Miss Beach's.
Although we often met at Joyce's parties I do not believe there
was the smallest degree of understanding between us.

Towards midnight Joyce would go over to the piano and try
running his fingers in a ripple over the keys. He would sing in
a light and pleasant tenor voice many Irish ballads in which

romance and lament and satire were combined, and which were the secret source of his inspiration.

Curiously enough one was aware of the reverberations of his fame even in these homely surroundings, for one was constantly reading critiques of his work in the numerous literary magazines, and also meeting writers and other intellectuals outside in the cafés with whom his work became a topic of conversation. Even Sola, the Spaniard, who had not one word of English, had heard that *Ulysses* was a masterpiece, and used to ply me with numerous questions about it—was it true that a character called Mrs Bloom had allowed her breast to be milked into the tea?

On principle Joyce refused to give any journalist a personal interview, and when I asked him the reason for this he murmured something about their always being anxious to misrepresent you. But I feel that his real reason was that he wished to remain mysterious and inaccessible. Whereas most artists are anxious for publicity, Joyce took great pains to avoid it. Yet in spite of the stiff barrier which he put against the outside world, he sometimes did unpredictable things. Once as I was entering his flat, I met a strange and very bohemian couple on the landing outside, just about to leave him, a shock-headed young man and a girl of the very type he professed to dislike. I asked him who they were since strangers with him were such an unusual occurrence. But he seemed uncertain of their names.

—What did they want? I asked him, piqued by my curiosity.

—They wanted to translate *Ulysses*.

—And you gave them permission?

—Yes.

—But you don't know anything about them. You don't know who they are, or what they are, I protested. Why did you give them your permission?

—Quite a number of people come to me and ask for my permission to translate *Ulysses*, he remarked, and I always give it to them.

—Always! I repeated, dumbfounded.

41

—Yes, he replied with a smile, because I know that none of them will ever do it.

And it was this remark more than any other which revealed to me his contempt for people whom he did not regard as serious artists able to undertake the sustained labour of an artistic work, ' people who sleep all day and amuse themselves all night ', as Hemingway put it.

Another reason why he so carefully avoided social contacts was that they might sap his capacity to work in that room of his which was full of books and old newspapers, and which no one was allowed to enter. Indeed in all the years I knew Joyce, I only saw him engaged in writing when one evening I walked in unexpectedly at tea-time to find him working in the dining-room behind the glass partition, the table spread out with manuscripts, each of them in a different coloured ink— the manuscript of ' Work in Progress '.

I sat in the Café Francis with him one evening, close to the glass doors swinging on their hubs, as a train of smart women entered in their furs and jewels, wafting a wave of perfume over us as they passed, presences of which he seemed almost unaware, and I began to wonder not so much what manner of man he was then, but rather what kind of man he had been. For when I consider Joyce's character I have always two different men in mind—the earlier Joyce, the Joyce of *A Portrait,* and the later Joyce of *Ulysses.* As I ponder over this, there comes to my mind the Joyce whom I had seen revealed to me in the small but significant article on James Clarence Mangan, published in 1902.

I have always known that he admired the strange and tragic personality of Mangan, not so much on account of his literary work, much of which is erratic and ill-written, and an acquaintance with which is not to be found far beyond his native island, but for his personality, his almost morbid singleness of purpose. Indeed it was while reading this article that I had first become aware of Joyce's duality of character, for though the article was written in a romantic vein and in a prose which shows the influence of Pater, he makes in it his first attacks on the very romantic mood which he himself was then expressing. So that I think even then his mind was conceiving the new realism which resulted from his experience of battling for a living in Trieste. As a very ambitious young man he must have suffered impatiently at the time he had to waste teaching English there. I remember that he once recounted to me, with some bitterness, an incident which occurred when he was giving an English lesson to a young Italian girl. Having finished the lesson Joyce was collecting his papers and was about to leave when the girl tapped him on the shoulder and pointed to the clock above his head—it wanted five minutes to the hour. Such incidents of daily occurrence irritated his haughty spirit and brooding on them turned him to cynicism.

But though he lived in Europe for most of his life, it did not interest him; his imagination was always centred in Dublin. He nevertheless had the fixed idea that if he returned there someone would shoot him. Indeed after all those years he would probably have passed through it unnoticed. But the idea of persecution seemed constantly to haunt him, and when I suggested that he should make a surreptitious return visit to see what it was like, he stared at me, grinning sardonically as though I were inviting him to commit suicide. He had been told that some man once called into a bookshop in Nassau Street and asked if they had a copy of *Ulysses*. On learning that they had not he remarked : ' Well, the author of that book had better not set his foot in this country again ', the momentary remark of some religious or nationalistic eccentric, as I pointed out. But as Joyce replied,

—It is just such an eccentric who does these things.

And Mrs Joyce backed him up in the decision, which confirmed him in his attitude.

IV

One evening we were talking about Russian literature and I was busy praising the Russians: Tolstoy, Turgeniev and Gorki, when Joyce said to me, with some irritation I thought, —Is there no English novelist you admire?

For the moment I could not think of any for my mind was too taken with the Russians and with my arguments in their favour.

—What about George Meredith? Joyce asked.

The stream of my thought was checked for the moment, then I said to him,

—No! Meredith is one of those authors I cannot read. I remember I came across a copy of *The Egoist* in the trenches and mad for something to read I was delighted with my find, but after a while, being continually reminded that ' he had a leg ', I became so irritated with it that I got some string and tying a stone on it I threw it over to the Germans. But there is a very fine English novelist to my mind.

—And who is that? he asked me.

—Thomas Hardy, I said. *Tess of the D'Urbervilles* and *Jude the Obscure*.

—But is not Hardy also something of a poseur, remarked Joyce, with his big butter-up of a dairymaid; the wicked squire with his curled moustaches and his dog-cart; her easy rape, and the sequence of the illegitimate baby; and then the biblical Angel Clare; their contrived misunderstandings, and that final drama of the murder; and Angel and Tess's sister standing outside the jail to see the black flag go up. To me the whole story is reminiscent of *The Murder in the Red Barn* or *The Woman Pays*. Also some of the writing is as clumsy as the plot, you must admit that. I always remember a sentence of his when he is describing Tess's feelings towards D'Urberville: 'and there was renewed in her the wretched sentiment which had often come to her before, that in inhabiting the fleshly tabernacle with which nature had endowed her she was doing wrong.' And again she says to Angel somewhere: 'the idea is unworthy of you beyond description.' Beyond description! I ask you! Then there is all that silly business about her supposed ancestral knights sleeping in their jewelled armour in their sculptured tombs. What a clutter of Victorian snobbery. And does it ring true, the whole story I mean?

—To me it does, I said, though I admit its clumsiness. But it is only a superficial clumsiness, for the underlying structure of *Tess* is sound enough, and Tess herself, in my opinion, is as fine as any woman in Shakespeare—in some ways she is finer and more human.

—It is more by a device than anything else, he replied, that she is made seem so fine, as you call it, for it is done by making the other characters seem venal: the seducing landowner, the weak Angel, the drunken old father, and so forth. It is the same device as the theatrical manager uses when he surrounds the leading lady on the stage with a plain chorus.

—Maybe, I said, but it works, which is all that matters, and there is always the richness of his language to support her and the originality of his detail which impresses because of the effort he makes to relate what did actually happen instead of polishing it off with a handy phrase: a persistence to say, or to try to say, what he intended to say, instead of fobbing you off with a happy phrase as so many authors do.

—But the murder! protested Joyce. It is contrary to Tess's whole character, for there is nothing in her make-up which leads you to think that she is a murderess. It was a gross psychological blunder on his part.

—She was an emotional type, poor, and a beauty, and the combination is a strong one, I argued.

Joyce shook his head.

—If you analyse his plots you will see that they contain all the tricks and subterfuges of melodrama, that ancient and creaking paraphernalia of undelivered messages, misunderstandings and eavesdroppings, in which the simple are over-simple, and the wicked are devilish.

—Maybe, I said, but those old-fashioned tricks, as you call them, are still effective.

—And then what about *The Dynasts?* he asked me.

He rose from his chair and went over to the reproduction *bois chêne* Breton bookshelf and took out a large green volume.

—Here it is, he said and, sitting down again in the chair, he opened it at the first page, and read it out to me.

—What does all that mean? he asked me, putting down the book, for if you can tell me you are a better man than I am. If ever there was a case of an author over-blowing himself this is surely it.

Then picking it up again he turned over some more pages at random.

—This is from a battle scene, he said, and he read out—

FIRST AIDE

The Archduke Charles retreats, your Majesty;
And the issue wears a dirty look just now.

—' The issue wears a dirty look just now '. Really, he exclaimed, it is just bad prose.

—I wouldn't try to defend it, I said, and I don't think anyone would try to. It is just one of those things. Hardy made up his mind to write an epic drama, for which he did not have even the ghost of a talent, or more important, the inspiration. That he was no poet we are agreed, but that does not prevent him from being a great novelist: the most serious of the English novelists, for he was not afraid to grapple life with both hands, different from most of the others who being commercially minded were over-anxious to entertain their readers and so became trivial.

—There was Kipling, said Joyce. There was something of the

46

artist in him in such a story as ' The Butterfly who Stamped '.
Also the *Just So Stories* have delightful touches of fantasy in
them, and it is that quality which seems to appeal to you.

—Yes, I agreed, but there was another side to Kipling which I
do not like.

—You mean that vein of crude practicability which runs
through him, like that of the suburban subaltern. I agree, and
then there is that jingling jingoism of his which must be very
offensive to foreigners.

—Yes, I said. Writers like Dostoevski and Turgeniev and
Gorki never presumed on their nationality. Surely that is the
mark of a great artist.

—I agree with you, he said, it is a damning trait, and it is to
be safe from the rabid and soul-destroying political atmosphere
in Ireland that I live here, for in such an atmosphere it is very
difficult to create good work, while in the atmosphere which
' Father Murphy ' creates it is impossible. At a very early stage
I came to the conclusion that to stay in Ireland would be to
rot, and I never had any intention of rotting, or at least if I
had to, I intended to rot in my own way, and I think most
people will agree that I have done that.

V

Joyce seemed very interested in the religious aspects of Tutankhamen's tomb, which we discussed shortly after its discovery on 26 November 1922.

—Whenever I walked through the British Museum, he told me, I was always impressed by the Assyrian and Egyptian monuments; those winged monsters with their cloven hoofs, mitred heads, priest-like faces, and long curled beards; and those Egyptian figures of birds and cats. It always occurred to me that both the Assyrians and the Egyptians understood better than we do the mystery of animal life, a mystery which Christianity has almost ignored, preoccupied as it is with man, and only regarding animals as the servants of man. I cannot remember at the moment a sympathetic mention of a dog or a cat in the New Testament, and I have always objected that the devils were transferred into the Gadarene swine. It is true that the parable of the lilies of the field touches on a deeper note, but one wonders why that parable was not taken further, and why the great subconscious life of Nature was ignored, a life which without effort reaches to such great perfection. Indeed since the advent of Christianity we seem to have lost our sense of proportion, for too great stress is laid on man, 'man made in the image of God', and I think that the Babylonian star-worshipper had a greater sense of religious awe than we have. But nowadays the churches regard the worship of God through Nature as a sin.

As I listened I was surprised to hear Joyce commit himself on religion, even as far as this, because in general he carefully avoided the subject. Indeed, I remember one evening meeting an Irish painter who had turned into a bitter anti-Catholic, and sitting in Joyce's room he had scoffed at what he had called this Italian conspiracy in which one of their number was appointed to represent God on earth. He had ridiculed the idea of man's creating God and enclosing Him in a tabernacle under lock and key to give Him only to those who were of the same sect as themselves. He had also attacked Confession as taking away God's power of forgiveness, and many other Roman Catholic practices, the details of which I have forgotten. Joyce was said to be anti-Catholic and I waited for him to express his opinion, but he retained his characteristic silence, his thin lips tightly compressed, uttering no word of approval or disapproval in the argument that raged between us.

The only comment I ever heard him make on these matters was his once telling me that when the new pope was being elected the conclave of cardinals were fed with less food each day so that in the end they were forced to overcome their personal jealousies and elect a pope, which, whether true or not, seemed to amuse him greatly.

His determined silence on the subject of religion and on man's survival after death, a subject which I often confronted him with, so intrigued, and even annoyed me, that one day, the subject having arisen between us as we were walking past the Odéon Theatre, I pushed him into a corner of the street, and I asked him the straight question,
—Do you believe in a next life?
Embarrassed by my sudden seriousness he quickly disengaged himself and with a shrug of his slim shoulders he answered,
—I don't think much of this life,
and closed the conversation, so that I realized that I would never get a direct answer on this subject from him.

Indeed, one of his marked characteristics was his avoidance of giving a direct opinion about anyone or about anything, and I attributed some of his reticence to his early life in the provincial atmosphere of Dublin, where everything one said was echoed back and forth with considerable distortion among

49

one's associates, until in the end it could assume the fantastic proportions of a Celtic myth, so that one was inclined to disbelieve all one heard. He so rarely expressed his opinion that his fundamental beliefs were very hard to gauge. In fact his mind appeared to be occupied to the exclusion of everything else with two main problems—that of human behaviour and that of human environment—and then only as related to Dublin. The surrounding French life with all its brilliance and attraction seemed to pass over him, and fed his talent only so far as he appreciated its intellectual freedom and its ' convenience', as he termed it. All he would say about Paris, when any one asked his opinion about it, was that 'it is a very convenient city ', though what he meant by this phrase I was never able to discover.

VI

Joyce seemed restless and ill-at-ease one evening, and I decided that he wanted to do some work or that he was bored with my company. I had already got up to leave when some remark of his about Russian writers set off an argument between us. I had told him earlier that the two literatures which I admired most were the Chinese, about which we know very little, and the Russian; and if I had to choose two favourite authors, one would be Lady Murasaki who, though she was Japanese, wrote in the Chinese tradition, and the other would be Pushkin, who of all the European writers is the one I would like to model myself on.

—Lady Murasaki I don't know, he replied, so I cannot give an opinion on her, but Pushkin! and he looked at me with a puzzled expression on his face. I cannot understand how you can be entertained by such simple fare—tales which might have amused one's boyhood, of soldiers, and camps, villains, gallant heroes, and horses galloping over the wide open spaces, and tucked away in a suitable corner a beautiful maiden of about seventeen years of age to be rescued at a suitable moment. I know that the Russians admire Pushkin, but, as I understand it, it is chiefly for his poetry which since I do not know Russian I cannot read. But I remember once reading a translation of Pushkin's prose, *The Captain's Daughter*—a bustling affair that might interest the Upper Fourth. As I say there was not a pin's worth of intellect in it, and I do not understand how you prefer him to the other Russians such as Tolstoy, who did much the same thing but on a grander scale; or Chekhov.

—Turgeniev looked on Pushkin as the greatest Russian writer, I remarked by way of an argument.

—You think that he was greater than Turgeniev then? Joyce asked.

—Yes, I do, I replied, for he was simpler, he was purer, and he was braver, and I think that all art, all writing, comes back to the man himself. I think that Pushkin was a finer specimen of humanity than Turgeniev. It is said that the Czar admired his wife and secretly wore her miniature, and that Pushkin's enemies, out of jealousy for his talent, or because of a personal slight, or mere impishness perhaps, sent him that infamous ill-scribbled note saying that he had joined 'The Honourable Company of Royal Cocu's'. And the over-gallant, over-impetuous, and over-proud Pushkin sent them a challenge, and they chose their deadliest shot to face him, his own brother-in-law I think it was, and three hours later the most brilliant literary genius in Europe lay dead.

—Yes, I always thought that he lived like a boy, wrote like a boy, and died like a boy, Joyce remarked.

I could not help smiling at his quip, even though it was essentially untrue.

—We have to remember the code of duelling that existed at that time, I argued, when men were very hot about their honour, or that of their wives. Still, I suppose Pushkin could have ignored the letter in the circumstances, or found excuses; but that would have been against his temperament for his chief quality was his eternal youth, in which the oldest things were reborn in wonder; bandits, maidens-in-distress, and his personal honour, all of which were the themes in *The Captain's Daughter*.

—I suppose it was good for its period, remarked Joyce, but I certainly would not take him for my model, for people have become more complicated nowadays and demand more than such simple excitements as bandits, gallant young officers, and maidens-in-distress. The modern writer has other problems facing him, problems which are more intimate and unusual. We prefer to search in the corners for what has been hidden; and moods, atmospheres and intimate relationships are the

modern writers' theme. Also, when you say that Pushkin was a finer writer than Turgeniev I am not sure what you mean. If you had said that he was simpler, then I might agree with you.
—Yes, simpler and finer, I said, it is much the same thing. Take Turgeniev's long short story ' Roudine '—it is one of his best stories, yet it has not the quality of *The Captain's Daughter* for, compared with Pyotr, Roudine is corrupt and weak. He even doubts himself. Natalia the heroine is not the ideal heroine that Masha is, because she changes in her affection after Roudine has failed to run away with her, though all things considered, he being poor and a wanderer, it was an honourable act on his part, rather than cowardice. Turgeniev's story, I admit, is more realistic and its psychology deeper perhaps; but Pushkin's conception is more ideal, more abstract as the painters would say, and it is the ideal which humanity loves. For instead of being immersed in psychological doubts, Pushkin's characters face circumstances with a youthful audacity which wins over everything, and that is why he is to be preferred to Turgeniev, in spite of the latter's subtlety.

Joyce sighed and poured himself out another glass of ' St Patrice '.
—Here we are, he said, back into a discussion as to what is ' poetry ' as distinct from ' literature ', to what is life, and what is a lie trumped up by the imagination : the difference between the perpetual adolescent and *homo sapiens*. And for anyone to try and write in the style of a Pushkin as you said you wanted to do just now, or even Turgeniev, seems to me to be like trying to paint a picture in the style of Greuze, or Watteau : a piece of historical plagiarism perhaps, but not contemporary literature. For you must be caught up in the spirit of your time, and you admit that the best authors of any period have always been the prophets : the Tolstoys, the Dostoevskis, the Ibsens—those who brought something new into literature. As for the romantic classicism you admire so much, *Ulysses* has changed all that; for in it I have opened the new way, and you will find that it will be followed more and more. In fact, from it you may date a new orientation in literature—the new realism; for though you criticize *Ulysses*,

yet the one thing you must admit that I have done is to liberate literature from its age-old shackles. You are evidently a diehard traditionalist, but you should realize that a new way of thinking and writing has been started, and those who don't fall in with it are going to be left behind. Previously, writers were interested in externals and, like Pushkin and Tolstoy even, they thought only on one plane; but the modern theme is the subterranean forces, those hidden tides which govern everything and run humanity counter to the apparent flood : those poisonous subtleties which envelop the soul, the ascending fumes of sex.

—Maybe, I replied, for I do not deny your influence on present-day literature, and that of all the other psychologists, even though at times I may regret it; but also I believe the *beau sabreur* still has his place in the world. He may not be very adult and he may not produce masterpieces, or attempt modern masterpieces, though when I come to think of it, even Hamlet was a *beau sabreur manqué*. In fact in that very trait lies his greatness, for his tragedy is that he is a hero hampered by thought. And much modern literature is Hamlet-like in character in that action is overcome by thought which leads to pessimism.

But Joyce seemed to tire of the argument and, turning the conversation, he asked me :

—What literary personalities would you like to have known?

—You mean within recent years? I asked him.

—Yes, in recent years.

—The great Russians, I said, Pushkin, Turgeniev, and Chekhov.

—And Tolstoy? he enquired.

—Yes, I would have been anxious to know him, I admitted, though I don't think that I would have liked him. He was too fierce a man. Also at the end he became too socially minded, but I have to recognize the great artist in him, the writer of some of the best short stories ever written. I could not have loved him, but I could have admired him, for we do not love people who overwhelm us; and to me he is the ' Ivan the Terrible ' of literature, brilliant, kingly, and cruel, for no matter how charming he seems to be, underneath we feel that he is hiding something unpleasant and ruthless; and though one cannot but admire his talent yet he does not touch us the way Turgeniev does. Indeed, whenever I think of Russian literature, I think of Turgeniev's *Collection of Gentlemen,* and there comes into my mind that beautiful girl, Liza: her pride, her seriousness, and her inward conflict. The story flows on as inevitably as life itself, and as imperceptibly. 'Une jeune fille grande, svelte avec de beaux cheveux noirs', that is the only description he gives of her. He lets you fashion her according to your desire and imagination, and her emotions become your emotions.

—You have odd tastes, remarked Joyce, for I think that it is his weakest work, with the indecisive 'cocu' Lavretzky, and the anaemic cloistered Liza; and all that eccentric collection of aunts, uncles and cousins, who hedge her in in a novel which tasted to me like a literary seidlitz-powder, in which if I remember rightly they are always shutting themselves up in their rooms for knitting and devotions; and their one relaxation is an occasional carriage drive through the country when they sit around a lake and sigh, and then hurry home in case someone should catch a cold: the ineffectual life of farmers who refuse to work on their land. And again, the novel ends in the smoke it began in, when she decides to go into a convent . . .

—That is hardly a fair summary, I protested. Liza may not have the *élan* of some of the French heroines, or the brilliance of the Duchess Sanseverina in *La Chartreuse de Parme,* for instance, for the Duchess is more beautifully and exceptionally passionate; but we feel that Liza is animated with an inner spiritual radiance which is the fundamental difference between the Slav and the Latin races. It is only towards the end of the book and in that scene in Martha Timofeevna's room when she kneels down in the blaze of candlelight before the icons that we begin to understand the real Liza—do you remember it?

—Yes, I remember it, exclaimed Joyce, and a fine piece of treachery it was, staged there for the benefit of that unfortunate 'cocu' she had kept waiting all that time. To me she has always seemed to be the quintessence of religious selfishness, of cowardice even, for she cannot face the scandal of running away with Lavretzky, nor can she leave the cotton-wool comfort of her home and live abroad with Lavretzky in exile. So she goes into a convent—'away with her to a nunnery'. Indeed, the only merit of that book that I could see was that it is one of the first attempts at psychology in the novel. But the whole story is written in such an old-fashioned style that it creaks. Her secret thoughts remain hidden, as does the real movement of her inner being; for he is like all the classical writers who show you a pleasant exterior but ignore the inner construction, the pathological and psychological body which our behaviour and thought depend on. Comprehension is the purpose of literature, but how can we know human beings if we continue to ignore their most vital functions? Turgeniev was a sentimentalist who wished to remain enamoured of his own sensualism. He saw life in an ordered fashion, in spite of his proclaimed admiration for revolutionaries; in fact, he seems to have taken a special pleasure in taming and defeating them, as he tames and defeats Bazarov in *Fathers and Sons* and, in contrast to Dostoevski for example, he was a nicely mannered Russian gentleman playing occasionally with fire but taking care never to get burnt. Tolstoy was a more sincere man in my opinion, for Turgeniev preferred his slippered ease and his literary circles to anything else, and the only people who are convincing in his novels are his anaemic gentlefolk. His interest was in isolation and not in action, and his world is a faded world of water colours. I admit that he was an amiable person, and you cannot help liking him as you like a weak but pleasant personality, but I cannot admire him as a great writer. I think his best work was those early *Sportsman's Sketches* of his, for in those he went into life deeper than in his novels, and reading them I get the impression of the confused and simmering cauldron that Russia was in the 1840s, before the great boil-over. And I always remember the answer a peasant gave to Turgeniev to explain why he was not married: ' Have you got a family? Are you married?' ' No, sir, impossible,

Tatyana Vassilyevna, our last mistress—God rest her soul—allowed no one to marry. She even went so far as to say before the priest, " God keep me from having to put up with that—I, I am a spinster and as long as I live I will stay one. And what is all this to-do about? They are spoilt, that's what they are; what will they be asking next? " '

And Joyce gave one of those sudden explosions of laughter which were so rare with him.

—And *Spring Waters*?, I asked him after a while, when his burst of humour had subsided.

But he shook his head in negation.

—It did not make much impression on me, so my memory of it is rather hazy, but I remember the young Russian, Sanine, and his love affair with that little sugar-sweet Italian girl, Gemma, a long and tiresome episode which even an artificially induced duel fails to bring to life. That ride into the forest and the consummation of their passion in the thunderstorm, that I thought as dated as an opera by Bellini.

—He was a classical writer, I said, and, in contrast to a man like Dostoevski, his sane and balanced qualities are out of favour these days. Nevertheless, they are the lasting ones. Dostoevski passes over us like a storm, and like a storm he will be remembered, occasionally—but there is a quality in Turgeniev which is as polished and firm as Maupassant was.

—No, said Joyce, sentimentalism is never firm, nor can it be; it is a trend of warm comfortable fog. The present generation cannot stand him, and do you wonder? Passion creates and destroys, but sentimentalism is only a backwash into which every kind of rubbish has been cluttered, and I cannot think of a single sentimental work which has survived more than a couple of generations. Crude force is better; at least you are dealing with something primary. His short work was best.

—No! he went on, after a while; the writer of that period I admire most is Chekhov. For he brought something new into literature, a sense of drama in opposition to the classical idea which was for a play to have a definite beginning, a definite middle, a definite end, and for the author to work up to a climax in the second act and resolve it in the last. But in a

Chekhov play there is no beginning, no middle, and no end, nor does he work up to a climax; his plays are a continuous action in which life flows on to the stage and flows off again, and in which nothing is resolved, for with all his characters we feel that they have lived before they came on to the stage and will go on living just as dramatically after they have left it. His drama is not so much a drama of individuals as it is the drama of life and that is his essence, in contrast, say, to Shakespeare whose drama is of conflicting passions and ambitions. And whereas in other plays the contact between personalities is close to the point of violence, Chekhov's characters are never able to make any contacts. Each lives within his own world, and even in love they are unable to become part of the others' lives and their loneliness frightens them. Other plays you feel are contrived and stagy; abnormal people do abnormal things; but with Chekhov all is muffled and subdued as it is in life, with innumerable currents and cross-currents flowing in and out, confusing the sharp outlines, those sharp outlines so loved by other dramatists. He is the first dramatist who relegated the external to its proper significance: and yet with the most casual touch he can reveal tragedy, comedy, character and passion. As the play ends, for a moment you think that his characters have awakened from their illusions, but as the curtain comes down you realize that they will soon be building new ones to forget the old.

—I agree, I said, he was unique; his humanity was unique and it is in a play like *The Three Sisters* that you feel it most. But since we are talking about Russian literature, what do you think of Dostoevski? Does he appeal to you?

—Of course, replied Joyce, for he is the man more than any other who has created modern prose, and intensified it to its present-day pitch. It was his explosive power which shattered the Victorian novel with its simpering maidens and ordered commonplaces; books which were without imagination or violence. I know that some people think that he was fantastic, mad even, but the motives he employed in his work, violence and desire, are the very breath of literature. Much as we know has been made of his sentence to execution, which was commuted as he was waiting for his turn to be shot, and of his subsequent four years' imprisonment in Siberia. But those events did not form his temperament though they may have intensified it, for he was always enamoured of violence, which makes him so modern. Also it made him distasteful to many of his contemporaries, Turgeniev for instance, who hated violence. Tolstoy admired him but he thought that he had little artistic accomplishment or mind. Yet, as he said, ' he admired his heart ', a criticism which contains a great deal of truth, for though his characters do act extravagantly, madly, almost, still their basis is firm enough underneath.

—' Vapour and tumult ', is how George Moore described him. ' His farrago is wonderful but I am not won . . .', and neither am I, I said.

—Yes, replied Joyce, but how could a man like George Moore, the Parisian, admire a writer like Dostoevski—Moore whose literary heroes were Balzac and Turgeniev, traditionalists like Moore himself with all the inherited weariness of the traditionalists. But there are people, and many people, who think that *The Brothers Karamazov* is one of the greatest novels ever written. Certainly it made a deep impression on me.

—Nevertheless, he is chaos, I said, the first of the great incomprehensibles who tried to illuminate chaos, but only made it more obscure.

—In some ways, perhaps, agreed Joyce, but as I say he created some unforgettable scenes. Do you remember when Alyosha goes to see his father after Dmitri has attacked him; his father's head is still wrapped up in a red silk scarf, and he gets up every now and then to examine his wounds in the mirror while he declares he will go on living as he has always lived, passionately, evilly; his pride, his boasting; his desire for the young Grouschengka, the strumpet and virgin in one.

—I remember, I said, being asked by a friend, a writer, his eyes burning with enthusiasm, what I thought of Grouschengka. But I did not know what to answer him, and it was then that I realized that Grouschengka and in fact all of Dostoevski's characters were unreal, so while I am reading him, I am asking myself all the time would any reasonable beings act and speak as they do; exaggerations larger than life; or to speak plain useful language, they are mad, all of them. —Madness you may call it, said Joyce, but therein may be the secret of his genius. Hamlet was mad, hence the great drama; some of the characters in the Greek plays were mad; Gogol was mad; Van Gogh was mad; but I prefer the word exaltation, exaltation which can merge into madness, perhaps. In fact all great men have had that vein in them; it was the source of their greatness; the reasonable man achieves nothing.

VII

Like everybody else Joyce was very interested in the Bywaters
and Thompson case of which the English papers were full in
December 1922, even the *Times* giving it a detailed report.
Bywaters, a young ship's steward, had known a Mrs Thompson
for seven years and was always writing letters to her when he
was away on his voyages, letters which she destroyed. But he
kept hers in which she suggested ways of poisoning her
husband, letters which were produced at the trial, and which
damned her.

Tragic though the whole affair was, it was not without its
humorous side. Mrs Thompson used to get her husband up in
the night to drink his ground-up electric light bulb. In one
of her letters to Bywaters, read at the trial, she said: 'I was
buoyed up with hope of the light bulb and used a lot of big
pieces. . . . Would not the stuff make some small pills coated
with soap, and dipped in liquorice, like Beecham . . . I know
I feel I shall never get him to take a sufficient quantity of
anything bitter.' In another letter she said: 'I used the light
bulb three times. At the third time he found a piece so I have
given it up until you come home.'

Bywaters was a fine clean-looking young man of whom I
saw a photograph in the paper as he was being led into the
Old Bailey, the detectives ushering him in with the exaggerated
care of a mother for her only child, to judgment and death. I do
not know why one has such pity for them, but I suppose it is
because it is the age-old battle between youth and love against
convention; though why they did not decide to run away
together is hard to understand. It seems that she had a good
job, and was afraid that if she ran away with Bywaters she

would have had to live on his small pay, a fear which seems rather exaggerated, for in the first place she might not have lost her job; and in the second place, since she was such an efficient businesswoman she would probably have got another one without much difficulty. But evidently she made up her mind that in order to remain respectable she must have her husband die. Bywaters seems to have been a simple sort of boy, gallant and chivalrous, according to his behaviour at the trial, when he seemed anxious to take the blame and did all he could to protect her: an over-sexed and unbalanced young man completely under her influence, who during his voyage brooded over what she had written to him. Something of his state of mind can be gathered from his collection of newspaper cuttings, some of which she sent him and others of which he had collected himself, cuttings such as: 'The Poisoned Curate', 'Women who Hate Men', 'The Battle of the Calves and Ankles', 'Chicken Broth Death', 'The Shadow Marriages', and so forth. No doubt he would have been willing to run away with her, but she insisted on murder. Indeed it seemed to have been an obsession with her, for she wrote in one of her letters to him: 'Yesterday I met a woman who had lost three husbands in eleven years and not through war. Two were drowned and one committed suicide; and some people I know cannot lose one. How unfair everything is. . . .' The ideal solution for her was for Thompson to commit suicide, but he seems to have been an unusually unimaginative sort of man who drank his electric light bulb with equanimity until he found large pieces in the mixture. He seems to have known that Bywaters was in love with his wife and that they were plotting against him, but I suppose he did not believe that things would come to such a pass. Undoubtedly he was fond of her, though she secretly hated him, but at times, with her woman's wiles, she managed to hide her hatred from him, for in another of her letters to Bywaters she wrote: 'I told him I did not love him and he seemed astounded' . . . and when Bywaters asked him to divorce her he placidly ignored him. It is suggested that Thompson used to beat her occasionally which drove Bywaters into a frenzy.

—The mystery man in the case is the husband, remarked Joyce, the immovable mass before the irresistible force so deeply bedded in his habits that anything outside seemed to him unreal; and of him we have no clear picture. But one thing I am certain of is that if all this had happened in France they would not have been executed, and I think that English justice was at fault in trying them side-by-side in the same dock, for if one was found guilty the other was guilty also, yet evidence against one of them was not necessarily evidence against the other. There was a certain vindictiveness shown there. After all she did not murder him: indeed she may, for all we know, have objected to his assassination and have been powerless to prevent it. It is true she had incited Bywaters, and had incited him for years, but that is not quite the same as actually doing it. It was a difficult case I admit, but I think it was gruesome and inhuman for the judge to try them the way he did.

—There is no doubt that he stabbed her husband to death, I said.

—I know, and like the mills of God, English justice grinds slowly but exceeding small, and yet I think everyone has been shocked by it; and what a terrible thing the law can be sometimes. Like everything else, it should be subjected to evolution as the French have done, even over-done as some think, and some of its implacability removed. I see that she once wrote him a letter in which she said that ' He [the husband] has the right by Law of all that you have the right to by nature and love ', on which the judge commented in his summing up: ' If that nonsense meant anything, it meant that the love of a husband for his wife meant nothing, because marriage was acknowledged by law ', while he remarked that ' Bywaters' letters only breathed silly, insensate, silly affection '. In other words, humanity meant nothing, and the law meant everything: right, I suppose, to a point, but there should be some tempering of the law to suit the difference between a brutal murder, and the act, for instance, of a woman killing her child in desperation, and then trying to kill herself—a double crime in the eyes of the law.

—I saw some photographs in the newspaper of the personalities of the trial, I told him, and the husband looked like a typical young Englishman, good-looking and not unlike Bywaters himself—in fact they might have been brothers—a type which seems to have attracted her. She was pretty, and quite an unusual character, the self-confident manageress of a dressmaking department in the city. From a photograph taken of them on their holiday together, all three of them, her husband seemed very fond of her, for he is lying with his head resting on her lap.

—There was no real evidence against her, said Joyce, in spite of all her letters saying she had given her husband this, and there was not a trace of any poison, glass, etc., found in his body, and it took Bywaters' six-shilling knife to finish him off. Also at the trial she swore she had given her husband nothing, and it was all fantasy written by Bywaters, for her mind was evidently full of the stuff she had been reading, while she wrote those letters to make her seem romantic in his eyes because in turn he used to taunt her with descriptions of his life while on his voyages. As a picture I can see it all clearly, exclaimed Joyce, Ilford—the dark streets with dim lights showing behind the yellow window-blinds, and from the distance a soft wind coming up with the raw smell of fish and chips on it, the Thompsons walking arm in arm under the trees when this young man suddenly dashes out and stabs him, her crying and wailing, and her search, or pretended search, for help. I can smell the English effluvia here—and it reminds me . . . yes . . . of the Strand, say, on a Saturday night, the huddles of people in the passage outside the pubs; the sudden fights; the traffic-weary streets; the arc-lights shining down on the muddy tramped pavements. I remember how I disliked it all and I decided that I could never have become part of English life, or even have worked there, for somehow I would have felt that in that atmosphere of power, politics, and money, writing was not sufficiently important. Also though there is plenty of legal liberty in England, in spite of all that may be said, there is not much individual liberty, for in England every man acts as a censor to his neighbour, while in Paris here you have the only real freedom in Europe, where no one gives a damn what his neighbour thinks or does, provided he does not make himself obnoxious. But in England everybody is busy about everybody else, which, except for an Englishman, is intolerable. In the Dublin of my day there was the kind of desperate freedom which comes from a lack of responsibility, for the English were in governance then, so everyone said what he liked. Now I hear since the Free State came in there is less freedom. The Church has made inroads everywhere, so that we are in fact becoming a bourgeois nation, with the Church supplying our aristocracy . . . and I do not see much hope for us intellectually. Once the Church is in command she will devour everything . . . what she will leave will be a few old rags not worth the having: and we may degenerate to the position of a second Spain.

E

VIII

I gave a party in my studio in the rue de la Grande Chaumière, to which I invited the Jo Davidsons and some American journalist who was staying ·with them, my friend Barlow, a Miss Vail, Lady Orde and the Joyces.

In the morning I went out on the Boulevard and bought some cakes, trying to get them at those shops where they are most eatable. I thought of going down to Rumplemeyer's in the rue de Rivoli and getting some of their famous pastries, but I decided it was too far to go. Also they were expensive. I had to buy some cups and saucers, and the rest of the morning I spent giving my studio a cleaning, which it badly needed.

It was a fine old place with a big window facing down on to a tree-covered courtyard, on the other side of which were the Carlarossi Studios. It had a big wide floor and a *soupent* above it where I slept, and it was heated, as all these studios were, with a stove, the round barrel type, with a long pipe crossing over the *soupent* and out through the wall. By filling it sufficiently I could at times get it red hot, for the heat spread up the pipe also, which went a dull red, and so in spite of its big window the studio could be got very warm even in the dreadful cold of a Paris winter.

The first to arrive was Lady Orde, who was married to a painter, and then came Jo Davidson, his wife Yvonne, and the American journalist, a busy little man whose attitude seemed to be that there was a take-in somewhere in all this Paris artistic life and his mission was to expose it.

Then came Rudolph, an old friend of mine whom I knew in London during the war, and who, having acted as a courier

66

for a travel agency, had been stranded in Paris. Some French-woman whom he had met at a party thought he had talent, and very nobly gave him a small allowance so that he could remain there and write.

Next arrived Anita, a girl of Irish and Polish extraction who was trying to dry the Irish rain out of her system; and with her that splendid-looking American girl I had asked at the last moment, who was half Red-Indian and half American, a cross between Venus and Adonis though gossip said that it was the Adonis in her which predominated.

Finally Joyce, the guest of honour, arrived with Mrs Joyce, and as Jo Davidson knew him and I was busy looking after the kettles boiling, I let him introduce Joyce to everybody, which was an up-hill task, for Joyce, having painfully gone through the formalities of an introduction, retired a couple of steps backwards and made no further effort. Though he was the essence of politeness, he appeared either to be bored by my guests or to be too shy to make an effort to overcome the initial strangeness.

Mrs Joyce on the other hand was much more sociable, but when he was there she remained glued to his side and her natural sociability seemed to desert her. Jo Davidson, who had more social personality than any man I have ever met, did most of the talking and kept things going, while I went about desperately, backwards and forwards to the gas-stove in the far corner fetching the boiling water etc., with all the worries of a host on my shoulders. While I was bent over the stove a knock sounded on the door and who should enter but the handsome blanchisseuse, who had called to explain about her earlier failure to arrive at the Bal Bullier. She was in her rough work-ing clothes, but seemed to want to come in, so I murmured something about helping me with the kettles. There was a pause in the conversation among my guests as the girl entered, and everyone concluded that I had an intrigue with her, which unfortunately was not true, and I returned more confused than ever to my party, offering and re-offering the cakes with a desperate bravado to people I had already offered them to. When I returned to get some more hot water, she had disappeared as unexpectedly and as mysteriously as she had arrived; this concourse of well-dressed foreigners was not to her liking.

Slipping past my guests I went over to Joyce to see if I could bring him into the company, for I was always expecting from him a sudden ebullience of the high spirits, wit, and violence which fill his books. But he remained impassive, polite but impassive, answering a query when he was asked one, but no more. In fact where he stood against the wall, behind the stove, he might not have been in the room at all. While I was with him the bespectacled American journalist came over in a business-like manner to talk to him, or really to interview him, and I drew aside so as not to interfere, since no doubt it was an important occasion for him, a much-read journalist covering Paris, to meet one of its most famous characters at a studio party. He moved to the assault, but Joyce stood before him in the same limp, apathetic attitude, plainly refusing to respond in any way, while the journalist made every effort to prize open this literary oyster, wondering perhaps if this was the same James Joyce who had penned *Ulysses* or had some other man been fobbed off on to him.

At last he had to give up, a defeated man, or what is worse, a defeated journalist. He returned to Davidson, shrugging his shoulders, and I overheard him say :

—There is nothing left in him. It has all gone into his book.

I could not help but be amused, remembering as I did how, one afternoon a little while before, I had been with Joyce in his flat and was about to leave when he suddenly asked me to stay, for he said that two editors of the *Little Review* were arriving and would I help him to meet them. I must say that the suggestion came as a surprise to me, for these two women, having crossed the Atlantic to meet their literary hero for whom they had already compassed so much, had no wish to meet him through a go-between. One would think that Joyce would have welcomed them with enthusiasm—but no, when they arrived he remained standing at the far end of the table, only answering them in monosyllables, trying to turn the conversation on to me. In fact, being used in this manner as

68

a buffer between them and their enthusiasm irritated them and in the end I fled. I am certain that a similar situation occurred many times over, for Joyce's shyness, or his extreme sensitivity, prevented him from behaving naturally to strangers.

It was now getting late and the studio was almost in darkness except for the glimmer from the huge window and the red glow of the stove, when I heard Joyce cry out my name as a soul might cry out in its pain in purgatory—and he came forward in the obscurity, putting out his hands in his semiblindness to feel his way. I was just in time to prevent him from putting his hand on to the red-hot pipe. Certainly parties did not amuse him and he had come there no doubt because I was the host. Now he was anxious to go, his debt of loyalty paid. As I escorted him to the top of the perilous stairs, trebly perilous for him on account of his bad sight, I wondered—as was natural, even as the American journalist must have done—' is this the man who has written the book which has shocked the whole world—the man who in *Ulysses* has described Bob Doran weeping in the pub about Paddy Dignam's death : " The finest man, says he, snivelling, the finest purest character "...'?

Truly, appearances are deceptive, for who would think that this slight and delicately built man with his smooth clerkly face, small pointed beard, with those strong spectacles glassing his weak eyes, was the most revolutionary character in this age of artistic revolutions? Indeed I realized that there was much of the Fenian about him—his dark suiting, his wide hat, his light carriage, and his intense expression—a literary conspirator, who was determined to destroy the oppressive and respectable cultural structures under which we had been reared, and which were then crumbling. Indeed, I remember his saying to me once :

—You know that there are people who would refuse to sit in the same room as me.

And, sensitive man as he was, it may have been the fear of suddenly meeting with such people who would cause an explosion that gave him that restless shyness.

Mrs Joyce did not seem to be quite so conscious of his difficult position. Indeed the only time she ever mentioned the subject to me was one day when I met her in the rue du Bac. She had been to see a priest about something—maybe it was to go to confession—and she told me the priest had said to her:

—Mrs Joyce, cannot you stop your husband from writing those terrible books?

But she replied:

—What can I do?

Indeed it was the only answer she could give, for what rebel worth his salt is going to be persuaded out of his course either by his wife or by a priest?

In all, she was more philosophical than he was, and was always ready to accept the worst with the best in the ordinary sense, a down-and-out lodging house or the table of honour in a restaurant-de-luxe. About people she was more difficult, though she managed to hide her true feelings, but in private she would let an odd phrase drop to show how deep her resentment lay. She could not bear deception or insincerity in any form, and just as one of Joyce's main defences was silence, she, too, had learned the value of silence from him, when the occasion arose. I know at times she used to revolt secretly against the artificiality of Parisian life, and once at a party, when the dancing had started in a very uncertain and self-conscious way, she exclaimed to me:

—If this was happening in Galway we'd all be out in a minute on the road kicking up our heels in the dust.

Her natural spontaneity never deserted her, except after Joyce's death, when, it seemed to me, she deliberately suppressed it.

His sister Eva disapproved of the marriage and believed that her brother, having got himself into a false position, could not get out of it. She told me of an occasion in Trieste when they were re-arranging a room in a new flat they had taken. Satisfied at last, they all relaxed, when Mrs Joyce picked up a pee-pot and placed it triumphantly on the highest piece of furniture in the room. Eva quoted this incident as an example of her sister-in-law's common origin, though I could not regard it as other than a Ulyssian touch. For my part I never experienced anything from Mrs Joyce but a natural refinement. Indeed, in the Joyces' home there were never any dirty stories told; even risky ones were taboo, and if anyone started telling them they did not last long as a friend. Again, one could expect a very cold reception from both Joyce and Mrs Joyce if one brought to their flat a casual girl friend one had met in a café as, indeed, I was often tempted to do. Your *belle amie,* yes!—provided it was always she—but a casual piece, no. Joyce's sensitivity was such that during the composition of ' Oxen of the Sun ', which takes place in the lying-in hospital, he was put off his food because his imagination was filled with half-born foetuses, swabs, and the smell of disinfectants.

IX

One day, in a state of excitement, I went to see Joyce. I had come across a volume of *Plutarch's Lives* and had been reading it, and all the time I had been wondering how it was I had not read or heard much about it before.

The volume I picked up starts with an account of Phocion which I did not read, and then of Cato the Younger, only part of which I read, since I was not particularly interested in either lawyers or politicians. Then turning over some pages I read about Antony, and it was he who captured my imagination for he seemed to me to be the outstanding figure of the ancient world.

—The history of Antony and Cleopatra, I remarked, is one of the greatest love stories in which passion dominates wealth and power; and finally there is their brave contempt for death.

—Yes, agreed Joyce, it is Christianity which has made us afraid of death, for men, nowadays, live in two halves in which their desire to live is tempered by their fear of death so that we no longer know which way to turn, and as a result both our public and private lives are smothered in hypocrisy. The pagans faced death as bravely as they faced life; ' one life one death ' was their philosophy. But I don't know why you have chosen Antony as your hero. Surely there were many better Romans than he.

—It is because Antony is my idea of a full man, I told him. I believe that he could turn straight away from a life of luxury and debauch as only the Romans understood it to the utmost hardship, eating animals and things which no other men ever had eaten, as he did, for instance, during his retreat over the

Alps. In fact the greater the adversity the greater the man he became, and in his lifetime there was no hardship and no luxury which he did not experience. And in Plutarch he found an author who was worthy of him. I admire Plutarch's account, it is concise, imaginative and clear. I have tried to read Shakespeare's *Antony and Cleopatra* since, but I got lost in its sea of words. There is a dramatic tension in Plutarch's account which I find missing in Shakespeare, for words can drain so much away. Life is clean, spare, and hard —or can be; and I can understand why men of action fling books aside as I have often seen them do, as something second-rate, something that they cannot be bothered with: just as I understand why they look with contempt on intellectuals and literary folk, and other life-tasters.

—You're just being emotional, said Joyce, and carried away by the exotic background of their lives which appeals to your romantic nature. You are talking like a philistine.

—Maybe, I said, but even a good writer must have a good deal of the philistine in him.

—Yes, to a certain extent that is true, he agreed, for an author must not write for the arty. There must be a sound basis of fact in his work. You said that the man of action pretends a contempt for the artist and writer. But that is a very superficial point of view, for if it were not for the writer their actions would be lost and forgotten in the dust that they created. It is an artist such as Plutarch who makes them live again: the men of action and men of imagination are the complement of each other. Nobody was more aware of it than the ancient Romans whose emperors, generals and statesmen were the friends of men of letters. Indeed, if they conquered a city they always sought to enter it with the leading philosopher or intellectual of that city, holding him by the hand to show their good intentions towards the people. Today we are less civilized. But I am still not clear about the original point you intended to make, said Joyce.

—What I have wanted to say was that the classical style still seems to me to be the best form of writing.

—Perhaps, but to my mind it is a form of writing which contains little or no mystery, commented Joyce, and since we are surrounded by mystery it has always seemed to me inadequate. It can deal with facts very well, but when it has to deal with motives, the secret currents of life which govern everything, it has not the orchestra, for life is a complicated problem. It is no doubt flattering and pleasant to have it presented in an uncomplicated fashion, as the classicists pretend to do, but it is an intellectual approach which no longer satisfies the modern mind, which is interested above all in subtleties, equivocations and the subterranean complexities which dominate the average man and compose his life. I would say that the difference between classical literature and modern literature is the difference between the objective and the subjective: classical literature represents the daylight of human personality while modern literature is concerned with the twilight, the passive rather than the active mind. We feel that the classicists explored the physical world to its limit, and we are now anxious to explore the hidden world, those undercurrents which flow beneath the apparently firm surface. But as our education was based on the classical, most of us have a fixed idea of what literature should be, and not only literature but also of what life should be. And so we moderns are accused of distortion; but our literature is no more distorted than classical literature is. All art in a sense is distorted in that it must exaggerate certain aspects to obtain its effect and in time people will accept this so-called modern distortion, and regard it as the truth. Our object is to create a new fusion between the exterior world and our contemporary selves, and also to enlarge our vocabulary of the subconscious as Proust has done. We believe that it is in the abnormal that we approach closer to reality. When we are living a normal life we are living a conventional one, following a pattern which has been laid out by other people in another generation, an objective pattern imposed on us by the church and state. But a writer must maintain a continual struggle against the objective: that is his function. The eternal qualities are the imagination and the sexual instinct, and the formal life tries to suppress both. Out of this present conflict arise the phenomena of modern life.

74

—In my Mabbot Street scene I approached reality closer in my opinion than anywhere else in the book except perhaps for moments in the last chapter. Sensation is our object, heightened even to the point of hallucination. You described Plutarch's account of Antony as concise, imaginative and clear. In my opinion it is more concise than clear or imaginative; what is really imaginative is the contrary to what is concise and clear.
—Also in regard to environment, or 'background' to use a literary term, the background of the classicists and romantics is unreal for the majority of men. It has no relation to the lives that most of us live and to the surroundings which enclose them :

> Ordure amons, ordure nous assuit;
> Nous deffuyons onneur, il nous deffuit,
> En ce bordeau ou tenons nostre estat.

as Villon puts it. If we are to paint the twilight of the human personality we must darken the landscape also. Idealism is a pleasant bauble, but in these days of overwhelming reality it no longer interests us, or even amuses. We regard it as a sort of theatrical drop-scene. Most lives are made up like the modern painter's themes, of jugs, and pots and plates, back-streets and blowsy living-rooms inhabited by blowsy women, and of a thousand daily sordid incidents which seep into our minds no matter how we strive to keep them out. These are the furniture of our life, which you want to reject for some romantic and flimsy drop-scene.
—I admit I prefer my illusion, I said.
—There you are mistaken, said Joyce, for the fact of things as they are is far more exciting. Eliot has a mind which can appreciate and express both and by placing one in contrast to the other he has obtained striking effects. It is true that one cannot shed the past completely and one must take both worlds into consideration, but the hidden or subconscious world is the most exciting and the modern writer is far more interested in the potential than in the actual—in the unexplored and hallucinatory even—than in the well-trodden romantic or classical world.

75

X

We talked about André Gide's *Voyage au Congo,* an account
of his experiences when he accompanied the Citroën advertis-
ing expedition into Africa. Joyce had a great admiration for
Gide; in fact he was the only French writer, or indeed the
only modern writer, whom I ever heard him admire with any
real enthusiasm.

I myself had looked forward to Gide's book very much,
for I thought the combination of Gide and darkest Africa
would be splendid, but I was greatly disappointed in spite of
the widespread interest which was shown in it. *Voyage au
Congo—carnets de route* is its title, so I suppose I should not
have expected so much. Still, think what Pierre Loti would
have made of it, for in a sense *Fleurs d'Ennui* was started as
notes in something of the same style, but how much evoca-
tion and art is in the subjects inspiring him. In Gide's *carnets*
there is a complete absence of art. They are journalism, and
rather crude journalism at that; notes, one supposes, which
were taken down from day to day and thrown into book
form, an unsatisfactory and lazy way of composing.

Leaving aside the searchlight he throws on the social conditions of Africa, which were a matter for the French Govern-
ment, I could not understand what literary merit Joyce saw
in this book, or indeed in Gide's writing at all.

I have another book by him, the first copy of the first
edition of *La Symphonie pastorale* which Joyce gave me as a
Christmas present.

—Read that, he said to me, and let it be your model.

But I cannot read it: or at least to speak the truth I have

man-handled myself through it, that tiresome over-written faded story. It is, I admit, subtle and even poetic in intention, but it is written in such a wandering and indeterminate way that one feels one is dragging a dead weight after one, it saps one's vitality, and one is irritated by the same faded literary personality who wrote *Voyage au Congo*. So I protested to Joyce about him as an example of a writer who had a big reputation but who was of no value.

Joyce sighed.

Then he said after a while:

—I suppose there are people who think the same about me.

—Ah, no, I replied. You have salt, much salt, whereas Gide had to scrape the bottom of the 1890s with its faded classicisms and drawing-room psychology to cover a page.

—He has a beautiful style, protested Joyce. What about *La Porte étroite*?

—It is his best book, I admitted. His only book.

—It is a little masterpiece, he said. It is as fine as a spire on Notre Dame.

—I admit that it has merit, I said, some merit, but otherwise I can see nothing in him but a literary *vieux marcheur,* not so big a figure as Anatole France, but just as deceptive.

Joyce sighed again, his habitual sigh of weariness at my contradiction. Our points of view were too far apart to continue the conversation, so turning to me he said:

—Then whom do you admire in modern French literature?

It was a difficult question to answer for I did not read much contemporary literature. Only one name came to me, an author whom I had so liked that I had taken the trouble to collect some first editions of his work in the belief that one day they might be valuable.

—Max Jacob, I said.

—Who? asked Joyce.

—Max Jacob, I repeated. I was reading a book of his only the other day, *Cinématoma,* lively and witty sketches of French life.

But I could see by his expression that he did not think much of Max Jacob.

—How did you come to admire him? he asked.

—Somebody told me about him and I found his book original and personal, with individual and interesting literary cameos, very lively and original.

—He has not much significance, replied Joyce, putting Max Jacob aside. But what about Proust? he asked. There is somebody, surely. He is the most important French author of our day.

I had only read the first two volumes of *À l'ombre des jeunes filles en fleurs* in the translation by Scott-Moncrieff. I had tried to read *Du côté de chez Swann* in the original, but I had found it too difficult and had got lost in the tangle of his sentences.

—They seemed to me to be much over-written, I said, and those long sentences of his. . . . He wore me out with his refinements.

—You should have given him more patience, said Joyce, for he is the best of the modern French writers, and certainly no one has taken modern psychology so far, or to such a fine point. I myself think, however, that he would have done better if he had continued to write in his earlier style, for I remember reading once some early sketches in a book of his entitled *Les plaisirs et les jours,* studies of Parisian society in the '90s, and there was one in it, ' Mélancolique Villégiature de Mme de Breyves ' which impressed me greatly. If he had continued in that early style, in my opinion he would have written the best novels of our generation. But instead he launched into *À la recherche du temps perdu*, which suffers from over-elaboration.

—Yes, I agreed, for I like him and yet I don't like him—and I remember him, and yet I don't remember him, for he sees everything through a veil, and his characters get lost in a sea of words. There is no sharpness about him; no noise even. His mind is one of the most noiseless in literature. And his snobism irritates me.

—He is a special writer, I admit, yet in spite of the fact that he writes about decaying aristocrats, I rank him with Balzac and Thackeray.

—I am sorry, but all those well-fed leisured people irritate me, I said, people isolated out of life to whom love seems more like a disease than a passion. Though you say that his purpose was to give as full an impression as he could, I feel that he lacks the necessary restraint that every artist should have and, as a pampered and over-delicate man himself, he luxuriated in his hobby and could not decide when to stop. What did he gain by this experimentation in style?

—It was not experimentation, said Joyce, his innovations were necessary to express modern life as he saw it. As life changes, the style to express it must change also. Take the theatre: no one would think of writing a modern play in the style the Greeks used, or in the style of the Morality plays of the Middle Ages. A living style should be like a river which takes the colour and texture of the different regions through which it flows. The so-called classical style has a fixed rhythm and a fixed mood which make it to my mind an almost mechanical device. Proust's style conveys that almost imperceptible but relentless erosion of time which, as I say, is the motive of his work.

—I believe he was an extraordinary man, as eccentric as his style was, I said, who no matter what the time of year was, always wore a heavy overcoat and dark spectacles and was muffled up to the chin.

—Yes, said Joyce, I met him once at a literary dinner and when we were introduced all he said to me was: ' Do you like truffles?' ' Yes ', I replied, ' I am very fond of truffles.' And that was the only conversation which took place between the two most famous writers of their time, remarked Joyce—who seemed to be highly amused at the incident.

—What about Barrès, Anatole France? I asked, but Joyce waved them aside with his hand without making a single comment on their work. Indeed I have been told that the nearest man to compare with Proust is Saint Simon.

—I cannot see the analogy, Joyce said, except that they both had this admiration—and in Proust's case one might say it was an adoration—for ' blood '. But in Saint Simon's case it was entirely political. He believed that the ' nobles ' or the higher aristocracy should govern the France of his day, and he was always intriguing for that purpose. Otherwise he had a totally different personality. Saint Simon was a realist if ever there was one, and his account of the intrigues, political and otherwise, of the Court of Louis XIV is written in a hard, dry, incisive manner without imagination or psychology even, but I suppose psychology was hardly of his time, for in those days they saw everything with a clear eye. Nevertheless he could give a masterly description, as, for instance, of the death of Louis XIV. I remember feeling very unhappy while I was reading those memoirs, that court atmosphere with all its unpleasant and spoilt personalities impinging themselves on me, and all those greedy harpies of women, and those arrogant and false men: the Duc d'Orléans, Saint Simon's patron, and his terrible duchesse, and that fat over-eating 'Monsieur', Louis XIV's brother. There is a description I remember of him coming to dine with the king, and he was so apoplectic look-ing that the king threatened to have him carried into the next room and bled by force. But that very evening on his return home he had a stroke, and there is a description of how he lies dying on the floor with only one unwilling valet present. . . . It was all very macabre, I thought.

—No man was less of an artist than Saint Simon, I said. Think of that court with its handsome women in their powdered hair and their jewels, their fêtes and their gallantries. Saint Simon seems to have been insensitive to it all or took it for granted, and his continued political hatred of the king's illegitimate children seems to have blinded him to everything else. Indeed in the whole book he has scarcely a good word for anyone except for the young Prince de Bourbon who died young from an accident out hunting when his horse stumbled and the pummel ruptured his stomach. It is one of his few genuine notes of regret.

—Yes, and there is a doctor Faquet, I remember, the Court physician, said Joyce, who used to hold long consultations whether he would bleed his patient from the foot or the elbow, a sort of *deus ex machina,* who killed off one member of the royal family after the other, though I daresay he prolonged their lives in some cases, since most of them suffered from over-eating. But I cannot see any relationship between Proust and Saint Simon, no—not even on the question of 'blood'; for with Proust, as I say, it had an almost mystic significance. Do you remember his description of the first time he met a duchess: an Irish prelate meeting the Pope could not have made a greater occasion of it, a wizened old dame, if I remember rightly, but whose tread sanctified the ground.

—It is a cult I cannot understand, I argued. As Bacon remarked: 'old gold is old family'. It all seems to me to be on such a material basis; while with genius on the other hand one feels it is a gift of the gods.

—I would not altogether agree with you there, he said. There must be some quality in 'blood' for it to maintain its position generation after generation: some strength and some wisdom. Also how often do we find that some nobleman was the patron of an artist, or a musician, even when the rest of the world did not take notice of him. Indeed some people think that the decline of the patron has caused a decline in art.

—It was only art of a certain kind, art which flattered them or their sensibilities: a Boucher, a Watteau, or a Fragonard, or a Velasquez with his royal portraits.

—That is not altogether true, he objected. Louis XIV patronized Racine, whose art was of an aristocratic type I admit, but he also befriended Molière. And the royal court of Spain favoured Goya until he disgraced himself by making friends with the French invader, even helping them to choose the pictures from the Prado to be sent to France, I believe. You must admit that patrons have played an important part in the arts. Indeed in many cases they would not have been created but for their help.

Indeed what was the constant tragedy of the *Quartier* but lack of money? One is constantly hearing of the desperate circumstances of artists. Take the case of Modigliani, for instance, who died on 25 January 1920. He lived in continual poverty, a poverty which in the end, you may say, killed him. I remember being in the café the evening the news came in that he had died in hospital, and only a little later we heard

81

that his poor wife had jumped off the roof of her parents' house. When I asked, rather stupidly, why she had done it, they all shrugged their shoulders and answered: *Elle était dans la misère*. For that seemed to everybody to be the complete and explanatory answer, *la misère*, a word for which there seems to be no adequate equivalent in English.

I had been introduced to Modigliani by my friend Sola. He was standing at the *comptoir* of the Dôme drinking a rum when, for something to say, I asked him why the artists had deserted Montmartre for Montparnasse, which was an ugly bourgeois quarter in comparison.

—Studios have become hard to get in Montmartre, he told me, for ordinary people who are not artists at all have found them cheap and easy lodgings. And then perhaps a new art requires a new district. The art of Montmartre is *vieux jeu*. Also there are the two big Academies around the corner where one can draw a model for a few francs. . . . *Enfin,* the change has taken place, and anyway it is easier to sell a modern picture in Montparnasse than in Montmartre.

A singularly handsome fellow with stout deep chest, Modigliani was already ravaged-looking, for poverty, drink and drugs had done their work. Nevertheless, in spite of his debauched appearance he still retained an air of distinction and of singular nobility, and even as I talked with him I remembered some of those fine drawings of his which I had admired in the windows of the various *marchands de tableaux*: a fusion of the Italian primitive and Negro sculpture, those girls of his with their slender necks, sightless eyes, and delicately etched mouths. Of the many there is one in particular which always stands out in my memory. It is of Madame Hastings, done in 1915 at the beginning of the love affair which was to become a legend in the *Quartier*. Drawn in pencil and crayon, it is just a head: her hair divided down the centre, the eyes blank and almond-shaped, the mouth small and full-lipped, the neck long and slender, with the black tags of hair hanging down from behind the ears on either side—the impression of a young woman in love. It was a drawing originally done for a sculpture perhaps, and one of the many he did of her at that time in which he recorded his numerous and changing reactions from love to hate, so that one can almost tell what were his daily, or even hourly feelings towards her.

It was by chance that I met her some time later after Modigliani's death, one afternoon on the terrace of the Café Rotonde: a small compact brunette, *bien roulée* as the French say, who spoke in a quiet voice tempered with disillusion. After I had told her how interested I was in Modigliani, I was delighted to be asked up to tea for the following Saturday at her apartment near the Lion de Belfort. She promised to lend me the diary which she had kept at that time.

As she poured out the tea and handed me the cups she complained about the failure of her literary ambitions. When she had first come to Paris she used to write a weekly article for a well-known English magazine, an episode in which a mythical young lady used to lose her clothes, with the subsequent adventures during the course of the evening to recover them. I naturally asked what she thought of Modigliani's work, and to my surprise she told me that she did not think much of it.

—Paris, she said, has many such fads and they quickly pass. He will soon be forgotten like the rest. He was a fashion in the *Quartier* because of the life he lived, but his work was too sentimental to have any value. It is the one thing we cannot stand, today—those sickly-looking women of his.

I was too dumbfounded and disappointed to make an adequate answer. Indeed, she seemed to treat the whole affair of her relationship with Modigliani as an episode of slight importance, she, who had been at the very core of Parisian artistic life, consorting with such remarkable personalities as Picasso and Utrillo. It had been an affair, she intimated to me, in which she had wasted her affection and her energy, and which had evidently brought her only disillusionment. The conversation veered around to literature, when for some reason, perhaps because Modigliani used constantly to quote him, the subject of Dante came up, and she remarked with bitterness:

—How could Dante, knowing as he did what life was like, have written that stuff about Beatrice and the Paradiso? All of which she evidently regarded as a bitter joke.

It was nevertheless with some excitement that I took back her diary to where I was living at the time, a studio over-looking the Parc Montsouris. Seating myself at the window in the fading light, I was prepared for a revelation as I opened the leaves of her manuscript, an account of their exalted if strained relationship, of Modigliani's doings and sayings, his dicta on art, and also of those sudden and unaccountable moods which seemed to pass over him like a storm changing the aspect of everything. But as I read on I was disappointed, for she seemed chiefly to be interested in Max Jacob's sexual abnormality, saying little about Modigliani except for a brief description of their first meeting: ' A complex character : a cross between a pig and a pearl : hashish and brandy : he looked ugly, ferocious and greedy. Met again at the Café Rotonde, he was shaved and charming . . .'. All very feminine and literary no doubt, but I did not feel the breath of passion stirring through the leaves. Indeed, even as a diary it would have been better if it had been written in a plain factual manner instead of in its rather artificial literary style. It might then have been an invaluable record of Modigliani's life during his most creative and emotional period, when she had lived with him and Max Jacob in *Le Bateau-Lavoir,* the famous ' Floating Laundry ', as it was nicknamed, in the rue Ravignan close to the Butte de Montmartre. This unique experience had made little or no impact on her. Either she had not understood its significance or—which is probably the truth—she had had neither the sympathy nor the talent to describe it. Now she seemed only to remember her lover's difficult character, the violence and drunkenness, which had submerged his finer qualities. Her general tone indicated that she had looked on him as another foreign *voyou* with whom she, an English lady, had got mixed up.

Shortly after Modigliani died I was taken up to his studio. It was a small single narrow room at the top of the house next to mine in the rue de la Grande Chaumière with a bare floor and bare walls and a single window with a small balcony. The artist then living in it was an Algerian, and very poor himself, so that there was practically no furniture in it, not even a bed, but a mattress laid on the floor, around which he told me he used to pour a little water to keep the bugs off. On the wall was hung the death-mask of Modigliani which some friends had taken in the hospital, with its sunken cheeks and indrawn lips, a very different face from the fine, robust-looking young man he had been. I asked who owned the mask. But the Algerian shrugged his shoulders.

—I found it when I came in here with the rest of the stuff. No one owns it. It is there.

But the thought came to my mind as I examined it, this shrunken image, how lucky was the man, a man like Joyce, who had a patron and so had been spared this calvary for if with increasing years Joyce had decided to abandon everything for his writing it might have happened to him. Though Modigliani had some artistic success, the appreciation had not been sufficiently general to save him financially. *Moi—moi—j'ai brulé la vie*, as he had exclaimed to me once . . . and what else in his hard circumstances could the poor fellow do? The demon of creation had entered him, and after that few men think of their personal safety.

XI

I had been thinking over our conversation about Proust, and it seemed to me that the nearest approach to him was the Japanese writer, Lady Murasaki, whose work Joyce did not know. I had recently come upon Arthur Waley's translation and found *The Tale of Genji* the most feminine book I had read, a meandering satire written in a steady monotone which never rises to a crescendo but at the same time distils an intangible essence, just as Proust does.

Lady Murasaki was, like Proust, a complete snob. To her, rank and position at Court were all important, and everything and everybody outside it was awkward and uncivilized, while the country she looked on as a barbarous place where youth and beauty waste their lives. She had no interest in achievement, for when the governors of the different provinces come to Court, all she notes about them is that they are rough and ignorant, and though Prince Genji himself is the principal Officer of the State she barely remarks on it, for it is his handsome appearance and masculine charm that interest her, and, perhaps more than anything else, his royal blood, for he was the illegitimate son of the emperor.

Her book is a question of style, and the pictures she gives us of the Court of Japan a thousand years ago do not differ so much in tone from the section of Parisian society which Proust describes. I had been wondering whether I should send the book to Joyce, and I talked to him about it at some length but my description was so confused that he evidently had no wish to read it. When I suggested lending it to him he almost ignored the suggestion.

—If you like, he replied in the most off-hand manner.

So I did not feel like bringing it. Pleasure hangs on such a fine balance that I did not want mine upset. Lady Murasaki's conception of life is so different from his that I am sure it would have bored him with its numerous complications and cross motives in which desire defeats itself, for in spite of his many successes Prince Genji is drawn in too many directions to be happy. Not that Joyce would have expected a happy hero, he was too tortured a man himself, but its aesthetic and romantic association would have irritated the realist in him.

I returned instead to the subject of Pierre Loti, in an effort to convince Joyce of his merit, but he could not understand my admiration for him. In fact my insistence seemed rather to irritate him and he said to me :

—If you must admire a French romantic writer why not admire a man like Stendhal with his *Le rouge et le noir* and his *La Chartreuse de Parme*. Passion was his *raison d'être,* and that surely is the religion of all romantics—exaltation through the passions.

—Maybe, I answered, but to be a romantic does not mean necessarily that you are cruel and ruthless, or even absurd as Fabrice often is. Loti was a romantic, a romantic impressionist if you will, but there is no ruthlessness, or cruelty, or absurdity about him.

—Maybe, but Stendhal was a product of the Napoleonic age, when the French saw themselves as world conquerors, and his attitude was such. But putting that aside one must admit that *La Chartreuse* is a good book in the romantic tradition.

—In a sense, yes, but it is not satisfying. It is too highly coloured for my taste even, and that long episode about Fabrice's incarceration in the Farnese Tower with the jailor's daughter Celia, a latin mixture of prayer and passion, throwing messages into his cell from her window.

—But you must admit to his merit, insisted Joyce, for few men have conveyed passion with such intensity as he has, as for instance in that scene in *Le rouge et le noir* when Julien hides in Madame de Rênal's bedroom: or again later in the book when he climbs up the ladder at night into the bedroom of Mathilde de La Mole. His description of their emotional frenzy is magnificent. And he wrote some excellent scenes, he continued, his unexpected praise of a romantic writer more and more surprising me,—like the one of the ball in *Le rouge et le noir* at which Mathilde becomes interested in Count Altamira for the singular reason that he was once condemned to death. Compare for instance Thackeray's social scenes in *Vanity Fair* with Stendhal's, how flat they are, yet their books were written about the same period and deal with much the same kind of people. Stendhal never became sentimental and soft the way Thackeray did, especially over women; in his greatest extravagance he remains hard and glittering.

—Agreed, but nevertheless, I said, perversely taking up the cudgels for *Vanity Fair,* it is a well-written book, and the characters are well sustained, and if they themselves do not develop much, their history develops in that subtle atmosphere of social assassination which you get in England. Thackeray has described the social life of his time in a broad and clear manner, but without pride, flair or brilliance.

—Yes, I admit that, said Joyce, but Thackeray has something which Stendhal did not have: humour.

—Humour, I exclaimed, it is that which has always prevented the English novel from rising to its full height.

—Do you think so?, interposed Joyce. What about Swift: and what about Bernard Shaw?

—They were not novelists, I said.

—Novelists or not, I think that there is something very inhuman about an author who has no sense of humour, and it is a thing which Stendhal lacked—and which some Frenchmen lack, their very emotional pitch prevents it, for they cannot but take life seriously, and no Frenchman will admit his inferiority before life. His vanity prevents it. But an Englishman is better balanced, and he will admit his powerlessness before fate by means of his humour.

—True, I said, but I nevertheless prefer Stendhal to Thackeray in spite of his confusion and obscurity for the reason that I prefer most things for their beauty. That is the quality we all admire in a work of art, not intellect and description of character, but beauty—beauty as you get it in Pierre Loti, in Turgeniev, in Mérimée. Indeed, to refer to your own work, I prefer your *Portrait* to *Ulysses* for the same reason—for its lambent beauty, its softly flowing phrases full of ascending lights, incandescent forms, and veiled images. It is the best description there is of adolescence, for the first of everything is the best. We are inclined to value experience too highly, but in all it is an ugly thing.

—It is the descent into hell, and *Ulysses* is that descent, for one cannot always remain an adolescent. Ulysses is the man of experience. Out of this marriage, this forced marriage of the spirit and matter, humour is created, for *Ulysses* is fundamentally a humorous work, and when all this present critical confusion about it has died down, people will see it for what it is.

—Then in your opinion, I said, the critics and the intellectuals have boggled the issue, have not seen your intention clearly, and have put meanings into it which did not exist, which they have invented for themselves.

—Yes and no, replied Joyce shrugging his shoulders evasively, for who knows but it is they who are right. What do we know about what we put into anything? Though people may read more into *Ulysses* than I ever intended, who is to say that they are wrong: do any of us know what we are creating? Did Shakespeare know what he was creating when he wrote *Hamlet;* or Leonardo when he painted 'The Last Supper'? After all, the original genius of a man lies in his scribblings: in his casual actions lies his basic talent. Later he may develop that talent until he produces a *Hamlet* or a 'Last Supper', but if the minute scribblings which compose the big work are not significant, the big work goes for nothing no matter how grandly conceived. Which of us can control our scribblings? They are the script of one's personality like your voice or your walk. And as for this beauty you talk about, an idea which seems to haunt you, one may say, in the terms of the new aesthetic of today, that 'only that which is ugly is beautiful'.

XII

One afternoon Joyce asked me to go with him to Larbaud's flat as he wanted to collect some books he had left there. Larbaud had lent Joyce his flat when he first arrived in Paris. It was a flat containing, according to Joyce, a room specially designed for writing which I was very anxious to see.

We crossed the Luxembourg Gardens and passed by the Round Pond in front of the Senate where there always seems to be a collection of small boys and girls sailing their boats, boats which seem to suffer the same fate as real boats, being wrecked around the base of the fountain, in the centre, or in collision with other boats, or entangled with rivals. Yet the French children never seem to show their annoyance openly or start those rough-and-tumbles that you see among English and Irish boys, and even among the girls sometimes. They treat each other with a cynical politeness which must date from the Grand Epoch and which, as Joyce remarked, is amusing to watch.

Mounting the balustrade steps we approached those big golden-topped gates opposite the Panthéon. Crossing the Boulevard St Michel we went towards the Church of St Etienne-du-Mont, and turning down a narrow street we stopped before one of those tall grey houses which you find in that quarter. Joyce took out a key and opened the door into Larbaud's flat. I have seen rooms designed for many purposes but never as yet had I seen a room specially designed for writing. It was shaped like the cabin of a ship, had a low, rounded ceiling with a light in the middle and a long table running down the centre with shelves like small bunks along the wall on either side at an arm's length. Situated where it was it would be cool in summer, and as it was small it should be easy to heat in winter. It was also sound-proof and draught-proof in contrast to the average room in a flat in which most writers have to work. But to my surprise Joyce told me that he did not like working in it.

—I don't like being shut up, he said. When I am working I like to hear noise going on around me—the noise of life; there it was like writing in a tomb. I suppose I would have got used to it, but I didn't want to because then I might have lost my ability to work wherever I happen to be, in a lodging-house, or in a hotel room, and silence might have become a necessity to me as it was, for example, to Proust.

Having collected his books and also some manuscripts, he put them into an attaché case and deposited the key with the concierge. Returning by the Panthéon, we re-entered the Boulevard St Michel and started to saunter down towards the river.

To my mind the Boulevard St Michel is one of the most attractive in Paris. Indeed in no other part of Paris were you aware of the distinctive spirit of the Middle Ages, and as we walked down towards the river our conversation turned on such men as Raymond Lulle, Duns Scotus, and Albertus Magnus, and the strange world they had created.

—Yes, it was the true spirit of western Europe, Joyce remarked, and if it had continued, think what a splendid civilization we might have had today. After all, the Renaissance was an intellectual return to boyhood. Compare a Gothic building with a Greek or Roman one: Notre Dame, for instance, with the Madeleine. I remember once standing in the gardens beside Notre Dame and looking up at its roofs, at their amazing complication—plane overlapping plane, angle counter-ing angle, the numerous traversing gutters and runnels, flying buttresses and erupting gargoyles. In comparison, classical buildings always seem to me to be over-simple and lacking in mystery. Indeed one of the most interesting things about pre-sent-day thought in my opinion is its return to mediaevalism.

—A return to mediaevalism, I exclaimed in surprise.

—Yes, replied Joyce. The old classical Europe which we knew in our youth is fast disappearing; the cycle has returned upon its tracks, and with it will come a new consciousness which will create new values returning to the mediaeval. There is an old church I know of down near Les Halles, a black foliated building with flying buttresses spread out like the legs of a spider, and as you walk past it you see the huge cobwebs hanging in its crevices, and more than anything else I know of it reminds me of my own writings, so that I feel that if I had lived in the fourteenth or fifteenth century I should have been much more appreciated. Men realized then that evil was a necessary complement to our lives and had its own spiritual value. I see that note constantly recurring among the younger poets today.

—There is nothing new in diabolism, I objected, it has always existed. You get it in Goya, and in Spanish literature, and it exists even in their gypsy music, while in France it re-emerged in the last century in Baudelaire and Rimbaud.

And halting in his step Joyce quoted to me out loud some lines from Baudelaire:

> Loin des peuples vivants, errantes condamnées,
> A travers les déserts courez comme les loups;
> Faites votre destin, âmes désordonnées . . .

—That, he exclaimed, is the new order of the day, and it is the constant strife between the two opposing types which creates the drama of the world. It was the intense consciousness of this battle which gave the mediaeval world its colour —the windows in Chartres Cathedral, the *Imitation of Christ*

He hesitated a moment and then said:

—And in my opinion one of the most interesting things about Ireland is that we are still fundamentally a mediaeval people, and that Dublin is still a mediaeval city. I know that when I used to frequent the pubs around Christ Church I was always reminded of those mediaeval taverns in which the sacred and the obscene jostle shoulders, and one of the reasons is that we were never subjected to the Lex Romana as other nations were. I have always noticed, for instance, that if you show a

Renaissance work to an Irish peasant he will gape at it in a kind of cold wonder, for in a dim way he realizes that it does not belong to his world. His symbolism is still mediaeval, and it is that which separates us from the Englishman, or the Frenchman, or the Italian, all of whom are Renaissance men. Take Yeats, for example, he is a true mediaevalist with his love of magic, his incantations and his belief in signs and symbols, and his later bawdiness. *Ulysses* also is mediaeval but in a more realistic way, and so you will find that the whole trend of modern thought is going in that direction, for as it is I can see there is going to be another age of extremes, of ideologies, of persecutions, of excesses which will be political perhaps instead of religious, though the religious may reappear as part of the political, and in this new atmosphere you will find the old way of writing and thinking will disappear, is fast disappearing in fact, and *Ulysses* is one of the books which has hastened that change.

—But America, I protested, there is nothing mediaeval about her, and her influence is going to be greater and greater as time goes on. She is going to produce a lot of literature in the next fifty years, in fact she is producing it at the moment.

—Political influence, yes, he agreed, but not cultural. I do not think that she is going to produce much literature of importance as yet, for to produce literature a country must first be vintaged, have an odour in other words. What is the first thing you notice about a country when you arrive in it? Its odour, which is the gauge of its civilization, and it is that odour which percolates into its literature. Just as Rabelais smells of France in the Middle Ages and *Don Quixote* smells of the Spain of his time, so *Ulysses* smells of the Dublin of my day.

—It certainly has an effluvium, I agreed.

—Yes, it smells of the Anna Liffey, smiled Joyce, not always a very sweet smell perhaps, but distinctive all the same.

—What about Walt Whitman? I asked.

—Yes, agreed Joyce, he has a certain flavour it is true, the smell of virgin forest is in him, and of the wooden shack, a kind of primitive colonialism, but that is a long way from being civilized.

—Then what about Thoreau?

—No, he said. I look on Thoreau as an American Frenchman, a disciple of Bernadin de St Pierre, Chateaubriand, and others of that school. He is not a real American in my opinion, he just carried the European *fin-de-siècle* passivism into the new world, that is all. Certainly he does not reflect the American mind as I understand it, the real American writers so far have all been minor writers, such as Jack London, Bret Harte, Robert Service in Canada and such like, and it will take a long time before they produce any art which is worthwhile. What they want in my opinion is a few more wars. Nothing matures a nation like war, for in war men are suddenly and violently brought down to fundamentals. Indeed some of the best art in the world was produced in conditions of war and by men who were also soldiers. Shakespeare, so they say, trailed a pike in Flanders, Cervantes was for years a prisoner-of-war in Algiers, and when he was not making fortifications for his patrons, Leonardo painted a picture for them.

—In Ireland we have had a lot of war, I argued, but it does not seem to have produced much art, in fact it stifled it altogether.

—Maybe—but you must remember that Ireland was never a highly civilized nation in the sense that Italy and France were. We are too far removed from the main stream of European civilization to be really affected by it, and as a result the ordinary Irishman never seems intellectually to have got beyond religion and politics. As a result we have never produced a large body of art in the wide sense—painting, architecture, sculpture. What talent we have seems to have gone into literature, and in that you must admit we have not done badly, especially in drama. The best English plays have been written by Irishmen, while in prose we have Sterne, Wilde, Swift (if you can count him as an Irishman), and then there is George Moore, according to you, and a few others.

—And now there is *Ulysses*.

—Yes—that is my contribution, and in it I have tried to lift Irish prose to the level of the international masterpieces and

94

to give a full representation of the Irish genius, and my hope is that it will rank among the important books of the world, for it was conceived and written in an original style. If we have a merit it is that we are uninhibited. An Irishman will seldom behave as convention demands; restraint is irksome to him. And so I have tried to write naturally, on an emotional basis as against an intellectual basis. Emotion has dictated the course and detail of my book, and in emotional writing one arrives at the unpredictable which can be of more value, since its sources are deeper, than the products of the intellectual method. In the intellectual method you plan everything beforehand. When you arrive at the description, say, of a house you try and remember that house exactly, which after all is journalism. But the emotionally creative writer refashions that house and creates a significant image in the only significant world, the world of our emotions. The more we are tied to fact and try to give a correct impression, the further we are from what is significant. In writing one must create an endlessly changing surface, dictated by the mood and current impulse in contrast to the fixed mood of the classical style. This is ' Work in Progress '. The important thing is not what we write, but how we write, and in my opinion the modern writer must be an adventurer above all, willing to take every risk, and be prepared to founder in his effort if need be. In other words we must write dangerously : everything is inclined to flux and change nowadays and modern literature, to be valid, must express that flux. In *Ulysses* I tried to express the multiple variations which make up the social life of a city—its degradations and its exaltations. In other words what we want to avoid is the classical, with its rigid structure and its emotional limitations. The mediaeval, in my opinion, had greater emotional fecundity than classicism, which is the art of the gentleman, and is now as out-of-date as gentlemen are, classicism in which the scents are only sweet, he added, but I have preferred other smells. A book, in my opinion, should not be planned out beforehand, but as one writes it will form itself, subject, as I say, to the constant emotional promptings of one's personality.

XIII

One evening the conversation turned on reputations, when I remarked how strange and varied they were.

—For example, I said, there are those men who have had a reputation for one thing when it was something else which they did well: for being a poet, when in fact they were good prose writers, as in the case of Lamartine.

—He was also a bad prose writer, remarked Joyce.

—Yes, I replied, except for one book.

—I cannot say that I know him very well, said Joyce, for he was not a writer who appealed to me much, with his exaggerated romanticism, his conventional mysticism, and his plethora of description, but I remember liking ' Le Lac '.

> *Aimons donc, aimons donc! de l'heure fugitive*
> *Hâtons-nous, jouissons!*
> *L'homme n'a point de port, le temps n'a point de rive;*
> *Il coule, et nous passons!*

I said, quoting a stanza.

—There is nothing original and sincere in that. It may be his best poem; at least it is considered so. Indeed the *Méditations* is, of all, the best volume of poetry he wrote. I read a good deal of his work because I am interested in him and because in my opinion he wrote one of the prose masterpieces of French literature: ' Graziella '.

—I remember, said Joyce, reading it a long time ago, a story about his affair with an Italian fisher-girl. My recollection of it is that it was a well-sugared piece of sentimentalism in which they continually *fondent en larmes*. Indeed what I

96

have always objected to about Lamartine is his fundamental insincerity.

—Maybe, I agreed, but talent is talent wherever it is found, and the strange thing about it is that a man can be the essence of sincerity but it avails nothing if he has not the gift, otherwise his work tastes like last year's fruit. But in the case of ' Graziella ' he was really stirred. And there is great music in Lamartine's prose: he was a lyrical writer, in contrast to what I would call an intellectual writer.

—I suppose you would call me an intellectual writer, interposed Joyce.

—No, not altogether, I said. Your early works were lyrical—parts of *Dubliners* are lyrical, *A Portrait* is lyrical, but *Ulysses* is not, and perhaps that is the reason why it does not appeal to me. Much of it seems to me to be over-conscious, and inspiration is what I admire.

—Depends on what you call inspiration, doesn't it? remarked Joyce, and it seems to me that you mistake romantic flair for inspiration. The inspiration I admire is not the temperamental one, but the steady sequence of built-up thought, such as you get in *Gulliver's Travels,* in Defoe and in Rabelais even. But Lamartine's writing was just a flood of sentimentality.

—And of poetry, I added.

—Of false poetry, he replied.

—That ' Graziella ' is not a great work I agree. It may be considered sentimental but it describes life as many understand it: the open air life on the shores of the Mediterranean. And it is in pleasant contrast to the modern books which are mostly urban, about the artificial life that is lived in towns and cities.

—That is because cities are of primary interest nowadays, said Joyce. This is the period of urban domination. The modern advance in techniques has made them so.

—It is degeneration, I said.

Joyce shrugged his delicate shoulders.

—A writer's purpose is to describe the life of his day, he said, and I chose Dublin because it is the focal point of the Ireland of today, its heart-beat you may say, and to ignore that would be affectation.

—But let us return to ' Graziella ', I said, for I do not see it as
you do, as a sweet piece of sentimentality. For Lamartine's
picture of Graziella is in all a straightforward one and yet in
reading it one is acutely conscious of the mystery of her being.
Indeed I think that the essence of a personality is more truly
given by a straightforward account than by the modern
pretentious effort to deal in mystery. In life we often sense
the mystery of a personality in a casual gesture rather than in
hours of careful observation. It is Graziella's unawareness
which reveals her to you. It is through the colour and tone of
his words rather than by any intellectual analysis that a writer
conveys his impression.
—About the use of words I agree, said Joyce. I know when I
was writing *Ulysses* I tried to give the colour and tone of
Dublin with my words; the drab, yet glistening atmosphere
of Dublin, its hallucinatory vapours, its tattered confusion, the
atmosphere of its bars, its social immobility—they could only
be conveyed by the texture of my words. Thought and plot are
not so important as some would make them out to be. The
object of any work of art is the transference of emotion; talent
is the gift of conveying that emotion. But I cannot understand
your admiration for the romantic. If ever there was an
exploded myth that is one.
—It persists, I replied, and will always persist.
—Maybe, but in realism you are down to facts on which the
world is based: that sudden reality which smashes romanticism
into a pulp. What makes most people's lives unhappy is some
disappointed romanticism, some unrealizable or misconceived
ideal. In fact you may say that idealism is the ruin of man, and
if we lived down to fact, as primitive man had to do, we would
be better off. That is what we were made for. Nature is quite
unromantic. It is we who put romance into her, which is a
false attitude, an egotism, absurd like all egotisms. In *Ulysses*
I tried to keep close to fact. There is humour of course, for
though man's position in this world is fundamentally tragic it
can also be seen as humorous. The disparity between what he
wants to be and what he is, is no doubt laughable, so much
so that a comedian has only to come on to the stage and trip

and everyone roars with laughter. Imagine how much more humorous it would be if it happened accidentally to some ardent romantic in pursuit of his romanticism. That is why we admire the primitives nowadays. They were down to reality —reality which always triumphs in the end.

XIV

I met Joyce by chance one evening in the Champs Elysées
and we sat down for a drink in 'Le Béri', with its scarlet
canopy and the straw-coloured chairs spread out over the
pavement. It was getting on towards six and the cars were
racing up towards the Arc de Triomphe. The sky was pale over
the roofs of the houses opposite and in front of us the boulevard trees were shimmering in that dark enamelled green
which is a combination of artificial light and daylight. As we
sat there on the terrace drinking our cinzano Joyce repeated
some lines from *The Waste Land*, which had evidently caught
his fancy:

> *O O O O that Shakespeherian Rag—*
> *It's so elegant*
> *So intelligent*
> *' What shall I do now? What shall I do? '*
> *' I shall rush out as I am, and walk the street*
> *' With my hair down, so. What shall we do tomorrow?*
> *' What shall we ever do? '*

And as he repeated the lines I found them irritating. Sensing
my mood he turned to look at me.
—I see that you do not care for Eliot, he remarked.
—I do not care for those particular lines, I said, though I
admit that he has written some excellent verse, light verse
such as ' Sweeney among the Nightingales '. But for me a
poet must be serious, I said, and remembering some lines out
of *Sordello* I quoted them to him:

Not any strollings now at even-close
Down the field path, Sordello! by thorn-rows
Alive with lamp-flies, swimming spots of fire
And dew, outlining the black cypress' spire
She waits you at, Elys, who heard you first
Woo her, the snow-month through, but ere she durst
Answer 't was April. Linden-flower-time-long
Her eyes were on the ground; 't is July, strong
Now; and because white dust-clouds overwhelm
The woodside, here or by the village elm
That holds the moon, she meets you, somewhat pale . . .

—Look at the seriousness of it, the weight of the emotion, the richness of the imagery.

But Joyce criticized it strongly.

—It is full of clichés, he exclaimed, which have been used by literary men ad nauseam—' strolling down the field-path '— ' the lamp-flies '—' the cypress' spire '—and the girl waiting for him in the wood, and refusing to give her answer in April —oh dear! Haven't we had enough of all that. It was written in a tradition that is dying—is already dead, one may say.

—But does tradition ever die? I asked him. What is art but the same formula used over and over again in a different way?

—Browning of the many words, replied Joyce, whose characters, no matter who they are, all talk like intellectuals: a mind that creeps along repeating itself endlessly until eventually he is lost in the maze of words. But did you ever hear anyone talk like Browning's characters? Or if you did, didn't you feel you were going crazy, or getting drunk? *The Waste Land* is the expression of our time in which we are trying to lift off the accumulated weight of the ages which was stifling original thought: formulas which may have meant something in the past but which mean nothing today. Eliot searches for images of emotion rather than for an ordered sequence, and in this he is related to all the other modern poets. Is it because he is not traditional that you do not care for him?

—There is something in that, I said, for I wonder if one can work outside tradition. What, after all, is tradition but the accumulated wisdom of the ages? Eliot has some good lines, I admit, and even whole verses. But the total man does not satisfy me.

—Does any total man satisfy us? asked Joyce. Certainly not the total Browning, if anyone could digest him. At least Eliot has not over-written himself as Browning did.

After a pause I asked him what he thought of Browning's great rival, Tennyson.

—Lawn Tennyson, he said, repeating the quip in *Ulysses,* the rectory prude, a poet deficient in intellect.

—At least he was not urban, like Eliot, I countered.

—No, he was suburban. It is not the wild countryside he writes about, but gardens. No, I do not care for Tennyson. Compare him with a poet like Donne, whose verse is a rich contrapuntal music which makes Tennyson seem as though he played with one stop. And Donne's love poems are more intricate, deeper than any others I know. To me he is very English, far more so than Tennyson, for the English mind, in spite of all that has been said about it, is intricate, and with Donne you enter a maze of thought and feeling. A poem of his is an adventure in which you do not know where you will end, which is what a piece of writing should be. In life you don't know where an experience will lead, and a work of literature should be the same. It is that which gives it the excitement. Donne is Shakespearian in his richness, and in comparison the famous French love poets sound trivial. He was a typical mediaevalist before classicism straightened out the English genius, for Donne and Chaucer were the two splendid geniuses in love with life before the puritans put out their ice-cold hands. Classicism was all right when it was paganism, but when it came to the Renaissance it had lost its purpose, and so it has continued miserably until this day, getting weaker and weaker until it has petered out in Tennyson, and in the stultified nudes of Alma-Tadema.

I was particularly interested to hear Joyce mention Alma-Tadema. It was the first time to my knowledge he had mentioned the work of an artist, for his attitude was like that of some other literary men who regard painting as an inferior art. Music interested him but not the plastic arts, and the only picture that I had ever seen in his flat, apart from his family portraits in which he had a sentimental interest, was Vermeer's picture of Delft. It hung over his mantelpiece, and he considered it a very fine work of art. I think one of the reasons, if not *the* reason, why he admired it so much was that it is the portrait of a city.

But in general he was not interested in modern art which was the rage in Paris. Picasso, Matisse, Braque, were names which never seemed to occupy his mind. I was, as it happens, more interested in painting than in literature and as a critic on the *New York Herald* I was constantly in touch with the art of the day. Often as we passed an art gallery in the rue de Seine, of which there are a great number, I stopped in front of them and asked his opinion of the latest Picasso, or Braque, but he would stare blankly at them, his face registering no interest or emotion, and would ask, after a time:

—How much are they worth?

I could not understand how he, a leader in modern literature, could ignore the efforts in another art which I regard as the most vital and exciting of our time.

The Russian ballet was also the rage, and I remember one of the early performances of ' Sacre du Printemps ' during which an uproar broke out in the audience. As I stood at the buffet afterwards I saw a girl pass through the foyer with her evening dress half ripped off, and remember thinking to myself that this was truly a civilized nation where their passion for the arts would take them to such lengths. When I asked Joyce how he liked the ballet he shrugged his shoulders and told me he did not care for it. He went once but never again. He thought the merit of the ballet exaggerated, an opinion so strange, and to me incomprehensible, that I doubted if I had heard him correctly.

In fact, he had a contempt for the multiple artistic activities of Paris. Either he did not understand them, or it was his bourgeois caution, a prejudice one might say, against anything new and fashionable which he looked on as a 'racket', a novelty which would subside as quickly as it had arisen.

His attitude to painting had a curious consequence, for one day he told me that he wanted someone to do a portrait of his father, to be painted in Dublin, and asked if I knew of anyone who could do it. I suggested Orpen, Paul Henry, and others, but he did not respond. Then I thought of Patrick Tuohy whom I knew slightly, a competent realist, but in truth nothing more. Joyce immediately decided on him because, as far as I could make out, he had known his father in Dublin, and so Tuohy was duly commissioned to paint the portrait which, when it arrived, turned out to be surprisingly good. Tuohy then proposed to come over to Paris himself and paint the rest of the family. I had been away over in Ireland but when I returned I found Tuohy installed, and every time I entered the flat I found him seated on the floor with a mirror in his hand touching up one of the portraits. But the situation was not a happy one, for he and Joyce jarred on one another, and no doubt Joyce resented Tuohy's continual presence. Tuohy could be very irritating, for he was nervously unbalanced. I remember his describing to me how he believed he had some abscess on the roof of his mouth which was poisoning his brain. I suggested that he should consult a doctor, but he replied that they could find nothing—They never can, he added hopelessly.

I do not know whether it was jealousy, that acid which eats into so many Irishmen, but he got the habit of constantly attacking Joyce. An unattractive, ordinary-looking man, provincial even to the point of being boorish, Tuohy may have envied this brilliant, international character. I know that I once invited him and Joyce to a tea-party at which there were some American friends. Tuohy had come up the stairs before Joyce and sat on a bench by the door, and when Joyce entered the room he started clapping in mock applause, which annoyed Joyce intensely. When some conversation arose about Joyce's work, Tuohy kept on interrupting from his corner saying: —Write a best-seller, that is what you have to do—write a best-seller.

Whether it was Tuohy's way of conveying that he did not like Joyce's work, or was a rude intimation that he thought that Joyce's work was written for sensation and money, I do not know, but the atmosphere he created was very unpleasant.

At that party Tuohy made friends with an American lady, and later, when he went to America, he stayed with her family as he had done with Joyce's. She wrote to me complaining that the beautiful Southern States girls had completely gone to his head, and that he had behaved in such an eccentric manner that, as she put it, 'no other Irishman need come down here for fifty years'. After that I did not hear from her for a year or more, when one day I received a telegram: 'Tuohy committed suicide in New York. Can you do anything?' But what could I do? I did not even know he was in New York. It seems that the poor fellow had pasted up his studio with newspapers, and then had turned on the gas. He was a fortnight dead before he was found.

When I told Joyce the news he showed no emotion.

—I am not surprised, he said. He nearly made me commit suicide too.

XV

Joyce once said to me, more or less in relation to his work:
' To fault a writer because his work is not logically conceived
seems to me poor criticism, for the object of a work of art is
not to relate facts but to convey an emotion. Some of the best
books ever written are absurd. Take for instance *La Chartreuse
de Parme,* about which you were complaining, the facts of
which no one could take seriously, any more than one could
take those of *Gulliver's Travels* seriously. Indeed, judging from
modern trends it seems that all the arts are tending towards
the abstraction of music; and what I am writing at present is
entirely governed by that purpose, for the more you tie yourself
down to facts the more you limit yourself. It is the spirit
which governs facts, not facts the spirit.'

I did not say anything at the time but thinking it over since
I realize how completely I differ from him, for facts to my
mind are far more wonderful and varied than any man's
imagination. Indeed it would seem to me that a writer's
purpose should be to follow the amazing sequence of reality
rather than to scorn it. A writer who ignores it, as Joyce has
done in *Finnegans Wake,* may startle us at first, but we do not
forgive him in the end, for he has ignored the hard core of
truth with which we are constantly faced. After all, the
universal man is not the intellectual man but the sensual man,
the man who gets his emotions, his very life from his contact
with fact.

—I do not think I know exactly what you mean when you say
' sensual man ', Joyce said.

—I mean the ordinary everyday ' Tom-noddy ', the man who

appears to be without purpose or ambition, who does a job to keep his body and soul together, whose pleasures and desires are those of his body, and whose chief interest is in his love-affairs, his personal comforts, and the pleasures he obtains from his emotional contact with everyday life.

—I do not attach the importance to him that you do, replied Joyce, for to my mind he is the putty which is moulded by men of greater intelligence and character than he has and he has no judgements except derived ones.

—Perhaps he has not immediate ones, I agreed, but in time he forms them and then they are irrevocable, and if a work of art has not that sensual element which is the substance of his life he will reject it. Take Hemingway. He seems on the way to the top because he is original. But his originality is a venal one, and what he writes about smells in life, and in time it will smell in literature too: stories about alcoholics and nymphomaniacs and people who live in a waste land of violence and who have no emotional depth. I admit to his merit, of course, that he is very much of our time. But in my opinion he is too much of our time, in fact his writing is now more the work of a journalist than that of a literary man.

—He has reduced the veil between literature and life, said Joyce, which is what every writer strives to do. Have you read ' A Clean Well Lighted Place '?

—Yes, I said, and it is one of his best, and I wish that they were all up to that standard.

—It is masterly, replied Joyce, in a glow of enthusiasm. Indeed, I think it is one of the best short stories ever written; there is bite there.

—But did you ever read Maupassant's *Bel Ami*?

—Yes, I read it a long time ago. It was an amusing and lively book, I admit, and I suppose it gave a good picture of the Paris of the 1880s among a certain section of society, but I could not call it a great work. Like everything Maupassant wrote it is in miniature. In fact I thought it read like a series of excellent short stories, but I could not take the principal character, Duroy, seriously—a sort of French studbull.

—He entertained me more than Hemingway's arena bulls, I

could not help replying. Also I dislike the climate of Hemingway's stories, that hard, crude, boozy world he writes about. And it may or may not be a personal prejudice, but I dislike a man swimming in liquor. Drunkenness is a subtle form of insult to everyone and to everything. It dirties the world more than anything else, and I get that dirtying in Hemingway's stories.

—Copulation doesn't affect you in the same way?

—No, I said, there you are dealing with a mystery which can become anything and transform everything. Love-making can end in love, it often does, and so its possibilities can be limitless.

—You do not agree with Aquinas then, that the act of copulation is the death of the soul?

—I suppose in the Christian sense every material contact is death to the soul, but since I am not a religious man I am not too certain what the word ' soul ' means. It can have so many meanings that I cannot decide which is the true one.

Joyce shrugged his shoulders, and turning away, picking up his glass, drank from it without answering, indicating, it seemed to me, that in his opinion it was useless to discuss such abstract matters, a waste of time even. So I decided to return to our original theme, the short story, and I said to him:

—It would not be hard to name some better short story writers than Hemingway: Mérimée, for instance. ' Carmen ' is a real *conte* in the French sense: concentrated, colourful.

—I agree that it is entertaining, said Joyce, but like so much that is French it is miniature in comparison with, say, Tolstoy's short stories. He was an unimportant writer, but at least I am grateful to Mérimée for one thing: he provided the story for the libretto of the best opera ever written.

That *Carmen* was the best opera ever written was hardly an issue worth fighting for and, having been snubbed over my hero, Mérimée, I decided to remain silent. On the whole Joyce was a very reasonable man, and it was only about three things that he was quite fanatical: the first was the merit of Ibsen; the second, strangely enough, the merit of *Carmen;* the third was the relative merits of restaurants, for a bad meal could sour his temper.

Indeed, it was over this last matter that a serious break occurred between us. It was in 1931 when he was staying in London arranging for his marriage, hoping no doubt that in the vast sea of human activity it would pass unnoticed. Living in a flat in a red brick built road off Kensington High Street he hated the whole atmosphere, accustomed as he had been to the continent, and above all Paris, and never did he seem so unhappy and lost as he did in what to him was now an alien atmosphere.

One evening I decided to call and take him in a new car, of which I was quite proud, to dine at a roadhouse on the Portsmouth Road, a place of some repute which still retained an old-fashioned character and where one dined in an oak-panelled room lit by candlelight, a place where tradition said Lord Nelson used to dine with Lady Hamilton. The meal was a bad one, I admit, and as the evening went on Joyce got into a smouldering ill-humour. In fact, I who had known him for so many years had never seen him in such a humour before.

When we got into the car to return to London I hoped that his anger, and also mine by this time, would have simmered down. But no, we only seemed to aggravate each other.

A heavily charged silence fell between us as I drove along the tree-shadowed Portsmouth Road, the mauve-coloured tarmac spreading like a ribbon before us, while I tried to remain as cool as possible, for I felt that this was a real break, which would not be easily healed.

As we had not seen each other for some time, for I was then living in Waterford, I suppose each of us had become reinforced in his own ego: Joyce a world-famous figure, and myself an unknown nonentity—in an obscure clash on the Portsmouth Road.

However, I did not feel like giving way to his ill-humour in spite of the fact that I was grateful to him for his constant kindness and interest all the time I had been living in Paris, much of the time on my own. I tried once or twice to re-start a conversation, but it died stillborn.

Then I suppose in an effort to be friendly again Joyce said in a low, intimate voice:

—I have just received very important news.

—What is it? I asked, thinking it must be something of literary importance.

—A son has been born to Georgio and Helen in Paris.

In truth I am not a family man who dotes on children. Also I was feeling very bitter at that time about the world in general. I had agreed with the remark Sam Beckett made to me that ' It had gone on long enough.'

—Is that all? I replied.

—It is the most important thing there is, said Joyce firmly, his voice charged with meaning.

A sudden suspicion crossed my mind; ' the most important thing there is' meant that another Joyce had been born into the world. Even to this day I am still in doubt, for Joyce's estimation of his merit would on occasion suddenly flare up to a point of madness.

Anyway, at the mere suspicion of it—for egotism has its limit—my bad temper rose up again and I said:

—I cannot see that it is so important. It is something which happens all the time, everywhere, and with everyone.

A tense silence fell between us as I drove to Kensington High Street. When leaving him back at his flat our ' goodbye ' was a very distant one.

However, in the years that followed when I was in Paris I called on him. But our relationship was never the same again.

The last time I saw him was when I called at his flat off the Champs Elysées, when we discussed the different reactions there had been to his work. As I was leaving he sank down on to a chair in the narrow hallway in that peculiar exhausted manner he had at times, and said with a sigh:

—I suppose my work is middleclass.

His remark surprised me, for what has art to do with class? In my mind I tried to trace back the origin of this remark, and the only one I could think of was a criticism of Joyce which had appeared lately in a book by Wyndham Lewis, an irritating piece of work with a strong political flavour to it, rabid and superficial.

—I cannot see what class has to do with it, I replied, for it occurred to me that few writers were less subject to class prejudice than Joyce was.

As I stood for a moment on the top of the stairs we both raised our hands in salute—a final farewell it was, though I did not know it. Then one morning in the early days of the war, the *Irish Times* rang up and asked me to write a short account of Joyce as he was dead. The news came as a thunderbolt to me and I turned away from the telephone with remorse and dismay. So much of my life in Paris had been bound up with him and Mrs Joyce, both of whom had given me a steady friendship as close as if I had been a member of the family. It had not ended, but had lessened as so many friendships lessen when distance puts its cold hand between them, damped as they are by circumstances and time, and by differences of personality. A personality can fuse with another personality for a time, but when that time is over we gradually re-enter the solitude of ourselves. Then all that remains is the memory of the fire which once warmed us both, and it is fragments of that memory which I have tried to reconstruct in this short book.